MY PRISON
HAD NO BARS

MY PRISON
HAD NO BARS

A child surviving alone in silence…

by James Lucot Jr.

MILL CITY PRESS

Mill City Press, Inc.
2301 Lucien Way #415
Maitland, FL 32751
407.339.4217
www.millcitypress.net

Printed in the United States of America.

ISBN-13: 978-1-54564-744-8

PREFACE

THERE WAS NEVER A PLAN TO WRITE ANY-
thing at all or even share any of this with anyone. <u>Ever</u>. Once
I started I just kept writing and writing every day using three
by five cards, legal pads, napkins, or whatever I could find
at the time — sometimes even at red lights. My sole motivation for taking this document to this level is the possibility of
helping a single person. I wish there was something like this
long ago for me. When I began to investigate books, memoirs,
personal accounts and other documents of abuse victims, I
found it very difficult to identify with the majority of what I
was finding. Most of the narratives were written by females
and the descriptions of the male victims almost always
involved, and rightfully focused, on sexual abuse histories

This is the account written as I remember experiencing it.
I have used the language I possessed at that time. I have not
gone back and added the psychological terminology for the
traits, symptoms and disorders that I later identified with
and educated myself about. I feel that process of self-explo-
ration is individual for every person and is a major part of
the learning and healing process. I do not want the reader
to come to any conclusion about themselves without fully
understanding the complete criteria and dynamic of these
delicate theories and diagnoses. Nor is this meant to replace
any therapy or assistance that they may need or want.

I have changed the names of those involved to protect
them and/or their families where applicable. I sincerely
apologize if someone feels uncomfortable by reading this

and I do not desire for that, but I have learned one constant from this process. There is only one truth and until the complete truth is accepted an individual cannot progress from their past. The secrets and dishonesty within one's self will never allow for growth and peace.

I sincerely hope that there is one person that my story may help, especially if they were alone in the situation like I was for so long. That was the origin and became my sole objective. I expended so much energy consciously and unconsciously throughout my life striving to rationalize and forget these incidents it became very difficult for me to recall these events in the detail that I want to. I tried to quantify and describe everything as best that I could. Many of my memories were fragments that began to re-emerge through the events of my adult life as a parent and husband.

I do not want anyone to feel sorry for me; that is the adult *"me"* speaking — but the *"child"* me is just the opposite. I know many have had it much worse and too many more are still in abusive environments right now at this moment. You are not alone, there is hope, and I truly believe that there is a positive in every situation. It may take decades to find it, but you can never quit. **Never, ever quit**.

My sister and I were the casualties of the war that my mother and father fought everyday of our lives.

This is my attempt to explain the unexplainable.

Background

AS OF THE DATE OF WRITING THIS, I HAVE been married for 22 years and have two children. I began my professional career as a registered nurse working on a liver transplant unit then I progressed on to multiple inpatient psychiatric units.

I decided to make a career change to education and been teaching advanced placement history for the last 20 years at the high school level.

My personal focus has always been on Holocaust Studies and I created an elective course that I have taught at the college level for the last three years. In my teaching career, I have received several awards, recognitions and accolades, but what makes me most proud is that they originated from the nominations by my students. Education and coaching have been an extremely fulfilling professions for me. I am very proud of what I do and has allowed me to continue to follow my own scholarly pursuits and interests. I have traveled to Poland and Israel on academic Holocaust studies. Currently, I am completing my second master's degree, this one in Holocaust and Genocidal Studies, on a full scholarship.

I am active in multiple alumni associations, volunteer in several historical and veterans societies as a speaker and facilitator, and at my daughter's school booster programs. By reviewing my resume, one might conclude that I have a happy life, a complete life with a distinguished career and content family. I am sure many people who know me thought the same, **but I was a keeper of secrets**, I hid myself in plain sight. No one really knew everything about me because I have been lying and acting my whole life.

That is what I was taught to do in my house even before I learned the alphabet.

Table of Contents

Chapter 1:

INTRODUCTION

"I always thought I was the only person in the world like me...."

"I WISH YOU WOULD DROP DEAD, YOU BITCH!!!"

THAT WAS THE FIRST THING, AND THESE WERE the exact words, that popped up in my mind when my son asked me once: "*What was it like when you were growing up, Dad?*" I have no memory of anything truly funny or pleasant that wasn't tainted in some way. My earliest memories involve screaming, threats, ugliness, silence, fear and sadness. I clearly can recall the yelling of the words *"BITCH"* and *"DEAD"* and *"GO TO HELL!"* over and over, in every room in our house and in many other different places.

These thoughts are very upsetting to me and repeat piercingly in my head whenever I recall them. Both of my parents were the children of alcoholics with extremely and both with severely disturbing enabling spouses, but that did not give them license to do what they did to each other in front of me. Watching him hit my mother and having both of them beat me, kick me and slap me were painful, but it was their words that resonated and hurt me more.

My earliest recollection is walking with my Grandfather on a summer day on the sidewalk in front of our houses. All

1

the houses in a row with the same size front yards bordered by hedges. He introduced me to an old man who asked me my age and I responded by showing him four fingers. As insignificant as that seems, it is very monumental to me. If I have any pre-trauma memory at all, that day would be it. Every conscious recall I have following that day is a collection of ugliness, unpleasantness and despair.

I was always afraid, and I knew that I should never talk about *"it."* I was being taught to deny the validity of any of my personal feelings and instincts. The charade of a normal family life is laced in my earliest memories. I do remember being terrified if anyone found out what really went on.

I never saw my parents hold hands, never saw them hug, never saw them exchange a gift, and never saw them kiss....... never, ever once. My father never told me he loved me but the times he roared ***"You'll never be a man!"*** at me were countless from my earliest memories until the day I left.

Never is such a strong, terminal word but in every description, I use it with the utmost cutting precision. I never even saw them smile at one another. I could not estimate how many times they embarrassed me, made me ashamed, made me lie, made me afraid and hoped that they would not be around, while simultaneously excusing them and making excuses for them.

Lakewood Street is a typical lower middle class, blue-collar neighborhood in the West End of Pittsburgh. A straight lane with cars parked on the curbs all the way up a slight hill. Row by row of turn of the century wood framed houses that were built side by side, many with multigenerational families living together, some with paid boarders living under the same roof with them. They all had an identical front porch that was the width of the house and that is where every sat in the evenings. My Grandfather used to say, *"it was the best room in the house."*

My entire extended family lived on the same block. My grandparents, both sets, lived one house apart which meant my parents, aunts and uncles all grew up together. They were

2

all laborers of some kind, almost all of them steel workers at the same mill, the E.L. Wiegand Plant. My great uncle was a supervisor and he secured jobs for everyone. When my parents married they bought the house on the corner of the same block that is the origin of my earliest thoughts. The houses were all built only a few feet apart from each other, but my family was only *"close"* by the physical location of the buildings.

Every child, especially a son wants his father to be a superstar, a hero, a role model – a *"Dad."* It has taken me almost a half century to realize and accept that my father did not have that as <u>his</u> goal. Family and children were never on his priority list. I think being a dad was something he checked off his list in his head and moved on.

He just wasn't a good guy. He might have been once, but not for me in any kind of consistent manner as a parent or nurturer. In public, amongst his friends and in the neighborhood, he could be the happiest and funniest guy. Entertaining and joking, the story teller and advice giver, he appeared to be the *"Dad."* My friends were envious of him and thought he was the man I wished for in my world.

Recently, when I attended my 30th high school reunion many of my classmates approached me and asked how my dad was and to *"Please say hello to for me."* I made up sensationalized stories idealizing him and creating a "super dad." I told those tales so many times throughout my life that I started to believe them myself. I made jokes and told funny stories about the scary times and the times he publicly humiliated my sister and I or my mother and repeated them over and over. Humor replaced the sadness, repetition chipped away at the memory and my dreams filled in the gaps.

Now I understand I was avoiding my reality and projecting my hopes all around me. Inside the house where we lived, alone just us, he struck a completely different personality. He was not a nice person and he could extremely mean, hurtful, frightening, threatening and violent. A thoroughly changed man with no compassion and even less affection.

His needs and his feelings were all that mattered to him and everything and everyone has a condition upon them. He "attached a string" to everything he did. He loved when people "owed" him and reminded everyone about it.

As a child, I was scared of him and wanted him to be nice to me. I wanted to be with him but the longer I spent with him the riskier it became. Like throwing matches near gasoline, it was only a matter of time before he would erupt. I always went back hoping for a different outcome. As an adult, I tried to build a friendship with him, but he was incapable of that too. I attempted to talk with him, get through to him, educate him and yes, just like my mother, change him too. She tried to change him from day one and he resented it and just became more oppositional and combative. There were so many theories that I would try, ignore him, praise him and compliment him trying to spark a feeling in him. All my attempts to try to make it into any type of relationship was just a cover up. A struggle to make it seem like it was real, but I always knew deep inside that a *"father-son"* relationship or connection wasn't possible, or maybe he couldn't or didn't want it.

Later, I realized that he is incapable of selflessly caring for another person. *Now years have passed, and it is sad, but I don't want it either anymore.*

Chapter 2:

SAFE

"Sometimes it is still hard for me today to understand how anyone could love me"

I NEVER ONCE FELT TRULY SAFE. IF I EVER GOT close to that, I knew it was temporary and finally, the hope it just stopped. Gradually, I realized that this was my life and it wasn't going to change. No one was going to stop it or come and rescue me. I had hoped that someday someone or something would make it all go away, and I could forget all the things I worked so hard to hide.

We lived in a small six room, two-story house on a dead end. The four of us including my sister who was younger than me by six years. He was usually out working or with his friends. Everything changed when he would finally come home. An hour before that the *preparation* started. My mother might try to organize things predicting how he might want them that day. As soon as his truck came down the street everything changed. My heart rate would spike when I heard his loud truck at the top of the hill. No two days were ever the same. Mentally we had to prepare to adapt to whatever mood he was in which most times was going to be negative. His fuse could be lit at any moment and everyone was always on two strikes.

He always came in through the garage to the basement, then the heavy, ominous footsteps of his heavy work boots on the stairs as he came up to the kitchen to eat. If he started yelling at my mother, we knew he was on the warpath. If it was later in the evening, I can remember being as quiet as possible praying that he wouldn't come in my room. My sister's bedroom was next to mine. Our beds were aligned, abutted along the same thin plaster wall that separated our bedrooms. When the fighting and threats started we would tap gently, quietly to each other on that wall. Back and forth, back and forth, we would make little sounds to each other. The tapping was the only thing that we had to know we weren't alone.

Sometimes when I was very young, before my sister was born, I would crawl underneath my bed and just lay under there. I can remember the bumps in the plaster pattern and I would connect them, count them, make shapes with them taking my mind away from my "real life." My pulse rate would rise and flutter with every creak of his steps on the stairs, every cough, every sound he made on his way up to bed.

Later, we would hide in our rooms after the arguing and screaming, and we would tap to each other. But some nights, nothing at all would happen. Maybe we watched television together or ordered pizza or had neighbors over. Just quiet, silent seemingly "normal," but just under the surface, my fear, my pulse rate, my clenched teeth, my body armored with my little hands formed into unconscious fists and my worry was still there, always there.

Our lives revolved around his mood and wherever that took him, took us.

He wasn't around much working swing shifts and overtime at the steel mill located across the city, then later when the mills all closed, and he was unemployed, he fixed cars in a garage in our backyard. When I was very young–before my sister was born–I have vague memories of laughing and a semblance of happiness, but I am not sure they were real occurrences or some images I may have created over the years.

Now, I wonder if that was part of many of the things I made up or hoped for in my mind. All the "nice" or "normal" memories include one consistent, one common denominator: there always had to be someone else there, an aunt or uncle, grandparent, friend or neighbor. He required an audience and we needed a witness. If someone else was present with us, this would greatly reduce his outbursts and mood swings.

There were nice times too when it was just my mother and I, but never when it was just the four of "us."

However, the scars that he inflicted, his denial of all the abuses he inflicted to me, the present validation of so many extended people that heard and/or witnessed it, the words on these pages and the wounds in my mind prove that it was all beyond real to the little boy I was then and the man that I am now.

Chapter 3:

FAMILY*

*This sense of <u>family</u> can refer to a group that con-
sists of parents and their children or it can refer to
a bigger group of related people including grandparents, aunts, uncles, cousins, etc. It is often
used specifically of a group of related people who
live together in one house. A group of people who
resemble a family in some way, a group of things
that are alike in some way.*

http://www.learnersdictionary.com/definition/family

*"The adults in my life, my extended "<u>family</u>" mem-
bers, knew what was happening to me and what was
going on in the house I lived in and they watched
me go back there..."*

AS A FAMILY, THERE WAS NEVER A TIME WE
all sat down to dinner. There would be food prepared in
some fashion most of the time, but everyone served themselves and ate wherever we wanted, and usually at different
times. My mother never sat down at all, ever. My father
would sometimes eat sitting in the bathtub, leaving the
dishes there as well.

When we were alone, the four of us, everything would
change. Long periods of quiet, no talking or interactions, just

sulking and melancholy. These periods would end with him going out of control and horrible words would be screamed, threats and physical contact would be made and then days of silence. Suddenly a nice gesture, or breakfast would be made, maybe a gift for me and it was understood that all was to be forgotten, forever never spoken of again. No discussion, processing or explanation given, no one came to my room and asked me if I was okay, but I knew that I was to act like nothing ever happened.

I knew at 5 years old that this was not normal, I knew other families did not do these things. My father never carved a pumpkin at Halloween, decorated a Christmas tree (although he would readily criticize the ones we decorated) or hid an Easter basket. I knew these things were not normal as well. There were too many times after one of his spontaneous eruptions where all of us sat numb, still with quiet perfection. He would just drop to the floor and lie face down. This could be anywhere, the middle of the kitchen on the brown and tan linoleum, hallway or living room, on the burnt orange short shag carpeting, with his big work boots on. He would have his eyes closed but not sleeping. It was more like pouting or a tantrum. We sat still wherever we were at the time. Terrified to move or speak out of fear that something might spur him on to round two. We would have to wait until he decided to leave, sometimes the time felt like hours, but I always knew not to move.

I was being raised in two worlds. One world was the "outside" world, outside of my home and one was our "inside" world, inside the doors of our home. There were two separate sets of rules and two separate set of expectations. In one world, I was always on the edge, under constant pressure, afraid of what would happen next. In the other world, I was afraid people would see through me and find out what my house was really like.

I can remember so many minute details of events that are so hard or too horrible to recall in their entirety. I can remember the hiding, I can remember the furniture and carpets, the smells, the make, model and the colors of his cars, but the whole of these events is still too much too grasp even so many decades later.

I have said many times before I became a father that I would never "spank" my own children. It was a flippant statement because in my mind I knew that I was never going to get married, never have children. That way I could protect "them" from ever having to experience a life like mine. That way I could stop what happened to me from occurring again. Looking back now, maybe I was afraid of myself in some way.

When my wife and I finally had our first child, our son, I thought that I had a complete understanding and was prepared to be the *"Dad"* I never had. I believed that I would be the father I had always hoped for myself. I was 30 years old. I had watched a few of my close friends become fathers. I felt that I had matured, and I knew that I loved my wife. I was excited and enthusiastic. I asked my wife to promise me that we would never have any profanity in our home. Our little boy was healthy and that was the only worry I had at the time. I was confident and felt I had enough insight into my past that I could become the parent I hoped and prayed for. I felt ready.

In time, I learned that my past and its effects on me were too powerful, too permanent. I found my father's words were coming out of my mouth, his anger was combusting inside of me and I became physical with my son. Nothing remotely like what was inflicted on me, but way more than I ever imagined, and it terrified me. Not with the violence or spontaneous eruption that I was forced to be the victim of and my son was 14 years old, and not 4 like I was, but still my hands were on him. The guilt, sadness, mystery and disappointment was, and still is painful to me. I apologized at the time, hugged him and told him that he did not deserve this behavior from me. I continued apologizing on and on, that night, days and weeks after.

My son is 21 years old now and a young man. He assures me that he doesn't lay in his bed at night thinking and wishing the bad thoughts about me like I did about my father. I don't feel the need apologize to this day, but I am still so very sorry. I still feel horrible even though I never did anything like my father did to me, but the subject is the same and that terrifies me to this day.

I hug my son every day, I tell him, text him and send him letters telling him how much I love him, how proud I am of him. I hugged him today as soon as he walked in the door. He is now taller than me. He is so much more than me.

My son knows almost everything about my past, although I leave out the details unless he specifically asks. I answer all his questions to the level he wants to know. His opinion of his grandparents was made already by the time I began this process. Later I found out he witnessed and heard things that I never knew about, but it introduced him to glimpse of what my world was like. He knows when I leave in the evening alone that I am going to my weekly therapy appointment and knows the reason why I need to go. Hopefully, what I went through has brought a positive in our relationship by motivating me and making me realize even more what I never had, what I want for him and me.

He is now in college far away, but when he calls me unsolicited it is truly a celebration for me personally. Once he and I were talking about how my father treated me, he stopped me and told me that we would never have problems like that and he hugged me…in a public parking lot. He is such a fine person and I am so very proud of him.

Many nights when he was a boy, I laid in my son's bed with him talking about his day, reading Harry Potter aloud to him and assuring him that he was loved more than anything. No one ever talked to me, no one ever read to me, no one told me that I was loved. And no one ever apologized to me, and no one ever came to help me when I was 4, 5, 6 and 7…

My wife doesn't understand how we could have been married for all these years and I kept all the pain and hurt hidden. Her quote to me was, *"Where did you put all that anger? You hid it so well."* She thought I exaggerated my past whenever I would lightly hint at truth, but in all my stories they would end with humor, satire or sarcasm which was my way of making my abuse history *"normal."* After all, my wife is very knowledgeable on the subject. She is an extremely accomplished child, adolescent and adult psychiatrist with a solid clinical background and established private practice.

My parents and extended family made me an extremely accomplished actor and well-practiced at hiding my past – even from an expert like my wife.

I haven't been the easiest to live with, and I am certain that I have caused more than my share of arguments and stresses in our marriage, but even my wife didn't see the truth about my hidden past as a long-term victim of physical, verbal and emotional abuse. I was that good, mixing lies together to make it more acceptable. I was that skilled in acting *"normal"* and covering up, that she minimized the facts that I attempted to soften with humor or a funny joke at the end. I had 30 years of practice when we got married, so I had told the stories over so many times with the inflection and *"punch lines"* at the end that I knew just how to weave them in without letting the truth out.

Our daughter, who is also six years younger than her brother, is very extroverted, assertive and happy. When she was 12 years old and playing softball, she would ask me why *"Grandpap doesn't come to (her) games?"* or why *"Grandpap says such mean things to Grandma?"* I try to answer those questions in an age appropriate fashion, but she knows. In time, I will tell her the truth too, because I am no longer hiding anymore.

I later learned from my children the horrible things he said in front of them, but I didn't know it for a long time. I was still living in the "charade" thinking that those behaviors were over.

I thought I was different, special, that I could handle anything he dished out at me. I thought I was Superman, and no matter he did to me, I could take it and more. Decades would have to pass before I began to realize and discover how wrong I was.

Chapter 4:

HIM

"He always made me feel that all the problems were because of me…"

SOME EVENTS OF MY CHILDHOOD ARE extremely clear. I wish that they were not. Saturday morning cartoons were a special time for me because it was my time, alone while my parents slept in or were gone. I had control. My thoughts could be taken away with *Scooby-Doo* or *Super Friends*. Those mornings were something that I looked forward to, and those memories, unlike so many others, were clear and painless.

Like so many children I had an attachment object, a blanket, *"my favorite blanket"* is what I called it. "My" Saturday mornings, I spread *"my favorite blanket"* out on the floor right in front of our Zenith wood cabinet, floor model television, and I would have a bowl of Frosted Flakes and let my mind roam away. I would cut the T.V. listings out of the newspaper and circle the whole line up of the cartoons I wanted to watch. I remember this as a happy childhood memory, one of the very few.

One Saturday, I spilled the bowl of milk on the carpet. I tried to clean it myself, but I was very young and of course, I made it worse and more noticeable. That was the last day I had that tradition. When he saw it, the fuse was lit, and he exploded. The screaming, crying, hitting and smacking followed, but what I remember most is his one threat that he screamed 12 inches from my little face. ***"When you grow up and have your own house I am going come there and take a shit on your couch!"*** I know I was not older than six when he screamed that at me.

Forty years later, I would relay that story to my therapist. I followed it with this simple and sincere question, *"Would that be an example of verbal abuse?"* I was serious, I wasn't sure if that met the clinical definition. I was always told that *"others have it worse than me"*, and that I *"didn't have it so bad"*, etc. When I saw her face change and focus on me, I realized how confused I was at that time.

My parents always yelled at me about how *"fortunate"* I was and *"how other kids had it so bad."* As an adult I had no idea what was **abusive** behavior and what would be normal. The physical pain faded, but those words still stab at me and return in my thoughts.

I spent the majority of my life trying to normalize that and so many other similar incidents and events. It is just becoming clear to me how the words and profanity he used about my mother and I, to me and in front of me were so nasty and abusive. There were racial slang names that I didn't even know were unacceptable.

I loved the television show *"The Brady Bunch"* as a boy. I hate it as a man. I watched that show and the repeats so many times, over and over consistently throughout my childhood. I truly thought that every family was like the *"Brady's"* but mine. I wondered how it would be to not have to consistently worry and not be scared. How it would feel to be treated humanely and to be heard. How it would feel to see parents love each other and care and support each other. That show caused me so much anxiety and sadness, but happiness and hope too.

I think back to that blanket; my baby blanket and I have memories of playing checkers with *"my favorite blanket"*, watching TV and building Legos on it, and sleeping with it. My last memory I have of that blanket was when I was 8 years old and I went outside to play. My father was in the driveway lying underneath an old car fixing it. The driveway was marked with oil spills and grease — and he was lying on my blanket. On the ground. Under a car. I remember looking down at him and our eyes made contact. No words were spoken, I guess I felt that I had to be tough and act like it didn't bother me. I walked away and never asked, nor was it ever addressed to me.

There are two facts that I can draw from that event and one of them must be true. One, he consciously took that blanket and destroyed it right in front on me to hurt me, control me and make me pay. Or, he had no clue and paid so little attention to me that he didn't even know or realize how important that blanket was to me. One of these must be true and both are so hurtful, the sight of him, the grease and dirt....it is branded on my memory to this day. Both of my children have their attachment objects which we cherished then and now.

My son had a stuffed little dog he called "*Puppy*" and my daughter has her baby blanket that she is sleeping with as I type this. These two items are treasured in our family. They have been to all our vacations and spoken of fondly, in photographs and memories. "*Puppy*" has even made a trip via FedEx back from Orlando, being overnighted by a very special night-shift, housekeeping supervisor after we left him in Disneyworld. It could have been a major disaster, at the very least a sad memory for a little boy. Today that is a nice story from our family history, one I hope my children will tell fondly — without having to edit it like I did with almost all the stories of my youth.

When I was 12, my mother, sister and my grandparents drove to Disneyworld in Florida because my father refused to take us. This was a huge undertaking for so many reasons, but we did it. I did not want to go because it was embarrassing to me. I knew that this was not how a "normal" family would go to Disneyworld and I knew that it would result in pain for me. After we finally arrived, checked into

15

a motel (without any reservations) my mother forced me to talk to my father on the phone. I did not want to do it and pleaded not to have to talk to him. We were in a Howard Johnson's Motel and I can still remember the pattern on the orange and blue bedspread. As soon as the phone touched my ear it started. *"Why are you doing this to me? Promise me that you will never do this to me again. Why do you want to hurt me? I hope you have a great time down there. Are you going to do this to me again? Are you?"* I was teary eyed and handed the phone back to my mother. I am not absolutely certain, but I think my sister was next up to get to talk to Daddy. There are a few photographs of me during that trip, no smile, no pose, just a *"take it and get it over"* with attitude.

Looking back, I realized that I never witnessed irritation or a *"small problem"*: my father never explained or modeled *"problem solving"* or *"discussions."* When a small issue presented itself all I ever saw was zero or 100 miles an hour, watching T.V. or violent rage, silence or war. There was no in between, there was no process or evolution, no steps or degrees just the "issue," then uncontrollable and irrational elevation to the highest levels. Then, too often it became verbally, emotionally and physically abusive. There was no precursor, no indicator just an instantaneous combustion of progressive yelling and threats.

For example, I had no "rules" as a child. In the summer I might sleep late for days, but if he decided that I slept in too long I could be shocked awake by him dousing me in the head with water as I lay totally asleep, soaking me and my bed. That happened numerous times. I complained to my mother she did nothing about that. Another thing I just had to accept and live with

I never developed a sense of dealing with different situations. When I became a father I literally had no concept of administering a "punishment" that remotely reflected the incident or behavior. I knew rage, I knew severe anger, but to independently address a consequence in an age appropriate nurturing fashion? That was an idea that was so foreign and unknown to me that I absolutely no comprehension of an effective reaction for a child's infraction. I used to joke that I had *"never been 'spanked' but I had been punched, kicked, slapped and thrown across rooms."* I wish I was joking. Another joke I used to say was that I knew that my father *"never read Dr. Spock's book about raising children because I never had a 'time out.'"*

As a parent, I realized that I never experienced a "punishment" when I was a child or teenager. I was never "grounded" or given a "time out" or "sent to my room." I never was consequenced in any consistent pattern or fashion for any of my behaviors. I truly had no idea what a normal reaction or consequence was.

The equation of how everything was dealt with in my house very simple, much like directions on a shampoo bottle, *"apply, lather, rinse and repeat."* But mine was more sinister. The sequence played out like this: a semblance of calm, verbal, emotional and/or physical abuse, being alone, then keep the "secret" and act like it didn't happen, wait until the next time because there definitely was going to be a "next time" and repeat.

I have realized that throughout my life I have unconsciously attempted to create a "relationship" with him that appeared "normal" to my friends and in public. I hoped that he would evolve into a "dad" for me. That he would become the *"Dad"* that I felt I deserved. Why I felt this might happen I have no idea now, but I hoped for it then.

Chapter 5:

CAN ANYONE SEE ME?

"I was afraid to talk to anyone out of fear what they might find out..."

I WAS A BED WETTER. OBVIOUSLY, I WAS extremely ashamed and embarrassed. The "accidents" weren't consistent sometimes weeks would pass without any incident. I had no control over it. A few times this occurred while on trips or other very inopportune places. The worst part was that he never addressed it with me ever. He made me feel so horrible. The fact that he never talked to me or comforted me made it much more painful. Never one time.

He made fun of me in front of other family members by teasing me openly, just by talking about it in front of them. His sister, my aunt and Godmother, whispered to me one time when I was about seven that she *"had that problem too"* and that was the only time it was ever addressed with me. He never associated with me when it occurred, never helped me and would ignore me with a frustrated and disappointed attitude. That behavior went on for years. He has never spoke to me once in my life about my bedwetting.

My mother asked my pediatrician about it and he suggested my parents give me a quarter each morning if I didn't wet the bed. Well, that was not acted upon and there were periods that I stopped bedwetting for days and weeks, but it always returned, and I would get so defeated. I begged her not to tell anyone, but she told many family members and friends, crushing my trust even more.

When I was 11, my hair started falling out in one large, silver dollar size area just to left of the top of my head. This resulted in a very observable totally bald circle on my head. People would ask me about it. My mother took me to a specialist who asked me if I pull my hair out and if I scratch my head there. I did neither of these things. My mother told me it was from *"wearing a baseball hat too much."* That was only thing I was ever told about it. Again, it was my fault. I couldn't understand why my hair was falling out on the top of my head rather than around the ring of the hat that actually touched my head.

I cried alone in my room so many times over these things. Why was something wrong with me? Peeing the bed and losing my hair...

As an adult I found out what the specialist actually told my mother. *"This boy is under a severe amount of stress."* My mother denied any knowledge of what that stress could possibly be. She changed the diagnosis to it being my fault for wearing my little league hat.

These symptoms and issues were screaming for someone to intervene in my life, but no one did. I hoped that my Grandma would just keep me.

I remember in the beginning steps of my therapy I tried to quantify or count the times he physically hurt me and/or my mother. I honestly can't recollect the specific occurrences to measure them. I concentrated and tried to recall those events that I had worked so hard to never have think about. I talked to my sister, I located former neighbors whom I hadn't been in contact with for in years and interviewed them, I even tried to talk with my mother. Then I realized it didn't matter how many times I was abused, how many times he abused her in front of me. I know that I mentally combined these occurrences together to make them more tolerable or maybe understandable.

And I know it happened. I know I was slapped, kicked, thrown, slammed. I know it was more than once, I know it still hurts me to this very day, and most of all, I know I did not deserve any of it.

When these memories surface, when I am triggered, I immediately and unconsciously respond with physical reactions. I flinch, tense up, perspire and grimace, clench my jaws and find my hands in fists. This can occur watching TV, at the movies, in public watching other people's interactions. I am also extremely easy to startle. My daughter and I solved it by her either texting me that she is coming out or gently walking around and entering my line of vision before she opens the car door when I am waiting to pick her up and by announcing when she is coming into a room when I am alone. My pulse rate flies when I am startled, and it takes time for me to calm down. This still happens multiple times a week.

So many of these memories and feeling came forth when I became a parent and it took me years to consciously realize it. I have that rage in me, I have the volume and anger in my voice and I have the desire to be physical and, why shouldn't I? It was the only example that I knew. He was only role model that I had. Unfortunately for me, my sister and my mother, my "teacher", my father, was very skilled in our many "*secrets.*"

I am not a "*tough guy,*" but I learned that I had to act like one, had to take on that persona to survive. Once as an adult I was driving home from work on a very nice spring day. I was in no hurry and I had no stressors of any kind. The road was four lanes with periodic traffic lights. While slowing down a red light I glanced to my left after I heard someone yell. The man in a car next to me leaned over across the lap of the woman driving and proceeded to elevate both of his middle fingers directly at me. I never have experienced "*road rage*" or any type of sensation like that before, but I found myself immediately pursuing the other car as it began to pull away. I can remember following him, but what happened next, I have absolutely zero memory of a conscious thought.

It just happened. If you were a mile down that major four lane road at the next red-light you would have seen me out of my truck, standing next to that car, reaching in the driver's window threatening and screaming at that man. I can remember standing in the middle of the street and I can visualize the other drivers looking at me, but I have no memory of opening my door or getting out of my vehicle. Behind me, my truck was in park, slightly ajar sitting in the lane with the driver side door wide open. I had never done anything like that before (or since), but I realized that I have his rage in me and no matter how educated, how much therapy I have, and how cultured or experienced I could become, <u>that</u> is still inside of me.

My father made me become a liar, an actor, a fraud, a sneak, a phony and sad excuse for a little boy. He made me a keeper of secrets, a pretender and something I was not supposed to be. He made me feel undeserving of happiness and responsible for all the problems in his, thus our existence.

Chapter 6:

THE TEENAGE ME

"I prayed and prayed so many times that it would just all go away...."

IN MY TEEN YEARS, I BEGAN TO ENGAGE IN "high risk behaviors" including drinking, staying out late, interactions with police resulting being placed on probation at one point. No one asked why? No interventions. Nothing.

The "father-son talk" (if talking to me in a driveway for 60 seconds could be called that) occurred when I had my first "girlfriend" in high school, but I didn't realize it at the time. I had no idea nor was I aware of what he was talking about until years later. I was leaving for a date with my girlfriend, whom I greatly cared about, but had no idea how to show it or had any role model to talk to for advice. I feel sad over that relationship because of how hard it must have been to deal with my silence, immaturity and my mood changes. I was scared, in a serious relationship as far as I knew, passionate in my mind but clueless in any manner of which I could have shared anything with her. That relationship lasted for almost two years starting my senior year of high school through my first year of college. She was my prom date, my first "love" and she deserved better. I thought I was so advanced in our "relationship," but I was guarded, immature, scared and childish. This was my first girlfriend and I didn't know what to do. I had no semblance of a role model, no support and no one to ask for guidance or interested enough in me to offer it. He did give me one piece of advice but at the time, I had no idea what he was talking about.

Every time I would go out I would have to walk down the driveway to his garage and ask to use "*his*" truck before I left. Usually he said nothing, made hurtful remarks or would put conditions on me such as *"you better check the oil before you take **MY** truck boy, and don't you forget it!"* while he was fully aware that I was showered and dressed. He never gave me advice or coached me how to ask a girl out or what to do on a date, nothing. One specific time he took me aside and spoke directly and sternly at me in a serious monotone whisper, *"you know…, if anything happens…, you can go downtown and for $200 and you can take care of things. You know what I mean."* I truly had no idea what he was talking about, I assumed it had something to do with getting a lawyer. Many years past until I figured out that my supposedly Catholic father was instructing me how to attain an abortion.

That was the sole advice I was given. I spun this into a funny story too and told it many times over.

This directive came to me with no explanation or education how one might become pregnant aside from teaching me how to go on a date, treat a girl respectfully or the protocol of meeting her parents. Honestly, television is what I copied, sometimes word-for-word, I drew on the fictional characters on *The Brady Bunch* and *Happy Days* as my dating guides. Later, I would use characters in books, Hemingway and Steinbeck stories, as role models for how I wanted to be.

Once he made this statement to me about marriage, *"As soon as a guy gets married the first thing he should do is punch her (his wife) right in the face just to let her know just how bad it could be."* He added this, *"any girl that grows up (in our town) will be a pig."* I was 16 years old and my sister was 10.

When I was in high school, I would use his truck. It was a 1973 Chevy pickup truck with no fuel gauge, no emergency brake, no speedometer, no horn, no seat belts and a stolen illegal state inspection sticker. I would never let my child near a vehicle like that aside from riding or driving in it. I made jokes out this too saying how I used to drive around in a *"$2000-dollar ticket waiting to happen."* On several occasions I found blankets, pornographic films, beer, *"roach clips"* for smoking marijuana in there. I doubt he smoked it, but the losers he associated with certainly did.

Once I pulled up at my Catholic high school parking lot and opened the door to get out while the Vice Principal, who was an extremely stern nun, was standing on the curb. She was a large, hard and tough nun. As I opened the door of the truck to get out, an empty beer bottle rolled out, loudly clanging. She looked at me, stared right through me. *"Mr. Lucot exactly where did that come from?"* she demanded loudly. I could hardly get it out, and I meekly replied, *"Sister, that is my dad's."* Nothing came out of that, no detention, no phone call home, she didn't even pursue it. I guess she had a clue of what my life was like.

Another time my father dropped me off at school for football practice in one of his hotrods, a 1929 Ford Roadster. The same nun was standing near-by. He floored it, peeled out and laid two long rubber black tire streaks in the parking lot. The nun came running after me, ***"Mr. Lucot!!! I want his name!!! Who was that?!!!"*** Again, I could barely get it out, *"Sister, that was my dad."* I never received any kind of consequence or discipline for either of those occurrences. (Twice as a teenager, I was driving in cars of his (both with illegal inspection stickers on them) that actually caught on fire while I was driving them. Twice.) The adage, *"a shoemaker's son has holes in his shoes"* was very accurate for me. Later, I would learn how and why he always tried to make us thoroughly dependent on him, to try to make us feel like children so we will always be under his control.

When I received my acceptance letter to college I became the very first person on both sides of my family to go to college. I proudly took the letter out to his garage to show my father. *"Duquesne University proudly accepts James D. Lucot Jr. to the School of Liberal Arts...."* He scanned it for a second or two. His response? *"Well, I ain't paying for no art"* and he turned around and went back to what he was working on. Not only was I hurt and deflated, but I kept going back over and over for his approval and kept getting emotionally annihilated. Every time.

As it was, I <u>paid</u> for my own tuition. I went to our local bank, ALONE, at seventeen years old, and sat down in an office. The bank officer was the father of one of my little league team-mates. He had me sign several documents borrowing the maximum amount of money possible. I had no idea what an interest rate even was. Since my father was technically "unemployed" I qualified for everything. I finished paying my school loans in my late thirties. So, ironically, **he** never paid for my *"art"* school anyhow. I repeated that tale over and over adding it to the "funny story list.

Occasionally, he would make me accountable on my whereabouts, but it was rare. I got into some small encounters that he really didn't punish me for, but I wasn't never "in trouble" like my friends were. He embarrassed me and made fun of me. The nickname he "jokingly" called me throughout my childhood was *"Horseshit Harry"*. He would use this moniker at different times in front of people supposedly teasing, but it was a *"bad word"* to me. There was an embarrassing line he would say when we pulled up in the car and he would race inside, *"The last one in is a nigger baby!"* Inside, I knew these things were wrong, but openly I laughed and tried to play the part, appease him and move on. Deflect, ignore and try to keep the waters calm.

I can remember so many events, times that should have been joyous and times that could be so rewarding that were ruined, crushed by his cutting insults, threats and screams or worse.

We would usually go to my Grandmother's house for Christmas Eve. When my sister was 16 my mother, father, sister and I took four different cars to my Grandma's which was only three miles away from our house. We all drove separately. Four vehicles so we all had an *"escape"* just in case.

How do I explain that? The four cars parked outside were not discussed by the rest of our family. No one asked why we brought four vehicles. It was understood I guess.

My senior year of high school should have been a great experience. We had our first ever football banquet in 1983 to celebrate the success of our team. We were one of the best teams in the history of our school. The banquet was a big deal, formal, awards and recognition, a very exciting and proud time in my life. When my coach introduced me that night he said that he *"wished that (he) could have me on the team for one more year"*.

Just before we left home my father ruined that night for me. The screaming fight he caused, the crying and threats in the minutes leading up to our departure. The silence all the way there in the car and then the sacred counterfeit smiles we had to plaster on like so many times before with red puffy eyes, just so we could walk in together and hide our reality. I hated that night. The event was brutally demolished for me, and I can never get it back.

Recently I told my sister that story. Her response was chilling to me. The same exact thing happened before her volleyball banquet....in college. He assaulted my mother before her banquet in 1993. Why? Because if he had to do anything that didn't evolve around him he could, and most often did, ruin it for everyone.

I was 29 years old when I decided to ask my girlfriend to marry me. This is supposed to be a special time between and father and a son where advice can be offered, celebratory memories can be made. I drove to my father's house where I grew up. I still needed his approval. Why? I guess I felt this might be the thing that will change him.

I walked out to his garage where he spent most of his time with his cars. He was underneath a car when I walked in. He was on one of those roller boards mechanics use. He slid out upon my request and looked up at me. I told him that I was going to propose to her. His response? *"So, what the hell do you want me to do about it?"* He slid back under the car leaving me standing there.

Stunned and saddened, I walked away and into the house. Now I went to mother just like I did as a child. I told my mother what he said. My mother looked at me and simply said, *"well, what did you expect?"* As I write this down I am not sure which of these statements is more shocking and hurtful, his degradation of me or her acceptance of it. He later followed that up with *"I hope you get a bitch just like I did,"* referring to my mother.

Did we stop this? No. We continued a bogus idea that this was acceptable, we ignored it and we placated him. Tolerance of his actions and words does not explain how we dealt with it. We rationalized and normalized, joked about it, ignored it, waited it out, all of it maybe just to survive emotionally and sometimes, physically too. For so long I thought I was protecting my sister from the abuse history, but I began to learn how she knew and remembered more than me. Once she told me she thought she *"was crazy"* and *"wasn't sure if (she) remembered things correctly."* I felt that way many times too.

Chapter 7:

THE CHILDHOOD GAP

*"I was taught that my parents were supposed to be
good, so then I must be bad"*

WE MOVED TO A NEW HOUSE AWAY FROM MY
Grandparent's street a few miles away when I was 4 years
old. There was a black steel frame table with a thick one-
piece, glass table top in the kitchen. I guess it could be clas-
sified as "modern." It was a rectangle and heavy. I know
at least two times, my father shattered that glass table top.
Once by slamming a two-liter Pepsi bottle through it. In
grade schools at that time we were forced to learn the metric
system. Pepsi and Coke began using large two-liter glass bottles at that time and we always had them in our house. I can
remember thinking about the glass *"Two Liter Pepsi"* bottle
as my teacher taught us about metric units of volume.

One morning I woke up to find the table with the glass
table top smashed into little glass cubes, much like a smashed
windshield after a head on collision, all over the kitchen floor.
I asked no questions and it was never discussed. I don't know
how or who cleaned it. Just like all the broken things in our
family it was swept away never to be spoken of again.

In the second grade, I brought my report card home
showing how well I did academically. I imagined that in
other homes this would result in a celebration. On this occasion, one of the very few when the scenes I imaged remotely

came to true. My parents smiled, it was nice. My father worked the 3-11 evening shift in the steel mill and the next day when I woke up the entire counter top in the kitchen was filled with treats, *Twinkies*, cakes and cookies. For years I held on to that memory, a small glimmer of a regular life, a sincere and thoughtful, selfless gesture by my father just for me. Recognition for my accomplishments and being thought of and cared about by him. Over 20 years later I overheard my father telling a story to a group of his cronies about how when he worked in the mill he rigged all the candy and cigarette machines, how he could steal the items from the machines. How he sold the cigarettes he got out of the machines and half price in the mill. I realized that he didn't **buy** those things for me for my report card. It was just another gimmick, a feint of one of the little positives that I remembered.

He never taught me to shave, to tie a tie, how to go on a date, swing a bat or how to throw a football. When I did receive gifts, they were usually something he desired or wanted me to want. A BB gun, a steam engine, go-kart–which were all nice and probably were costly for him, but they were **his** interests, not mine. Things he wanted and things that I never asked for. He never invested in me or for the person I was, we always had to conform to him. More than once *"my"* gifts did not come with the original box or directions. Just like the big screen television he brought home that did not have directions or an owner's manual. These gifts for me were *"hot,"* stolen and acquired by him from his co-workers in mill or from his friends in his old neighborhood.

The baseball glove I had in Little League was second hand given to me by a neighbor. I used it for years. When my daughter was playing fast pitch softball she didn't want a new glove, she liked using one of my old ones that was already soft and broken in. I insisted that she have her glove and bought her the same expensive model I always wanted when I was her age but never even dreamed of asking for or even possessing myself. While I was at the sporting goods store I thought of that as I stood there looking at a wall of hundreds of baseball gloves. I was looking at these gloves like I was a child, something that I could never have. Finally, I asked the salesman for another one. I bought one for myself too. We have matching black, Wilson model A2000 gloves, just like I always wanted. She was 12 years old and I was 49!

He never came to my games or practices. I needed rides to and from these fields and gyms, but when I asked him, that request was often was greeted with complaints or silence making me feel horrible. He often would make one of his lackies that hang around to take me or I would get a neighbor. I was not a priority nor was my interests.

I have attended every one of my children's Parent Teacher Nights at their schools. I know their teachers, assignments and tests, helped them with their homework and all the science and art projects. I volunteer at their schools, help coach their teams and I truly enjoy it. Currently, I am the booster club president at my daughter's high school. My father never attended anything of mine unless, on very, very few occasions, my mother made him. I would act like I didn't want him to come, make excuses for him, that *"he had to work,"* but I really did want him to be involved. Now, I see how my kids appreciate and communicate to me about my involvement. I know they like me being a presence in their lives and I do too.

I never order ice cream cones, only in a bowl or cup. That might sound odd, but I know it is one of my triggers. My father liked ice cream, so we would go to Dairy Queen sometimes. It was horrible. I hated it. It was an explosion waiting to happen. The countdown went just like this. He would lull us into a normal "family" event like getting ice cream. I can remember the server would ask me, *"What would you like?"* and I was too young to be consciously oppositional or defiant. I would respond a hot-fudge sundae or milkshake or whatever I really wanted. In his mind if I asked for anything but a "small cone" that would set him off. He would go crazy, ***"A cone isn't good enough for you?! You think you are so special! God damned spoiled brat!"*** Screaming and yelling, never letting up, threating never to take me again, scaring me and calling me names that I didn't understand. Making me feel so sad, horrible, empty, hollow and alone. Then the silence. Total silence for the ride home, for the rest of the evening, next day or days.

So, I never order ice cream cones. **Ever.**

My grade school did not have an actual cafeteria. We ate lunch in our classroom and we had to bring our lunches from home with us to school each day. Sometimes there would be fights and arguments in my house because there wasn't food to "make a lunch" with or my father would have eaten whatever my mother planned to give us. Sometimes, my mother would call a relative and ask them to make a lunch for me too. When their fights would go for days of screaming and silence, isolating and leaving, I guess the thoughts of my school lunch were not high on the priority list.

Once when I was in fifth grade, I went to school with no lunch at all. It wasn't not having anything to eat being the issue, but the other kids seeing me with nothing to eat terrified me. I remember being so scared in the morning that someone would find out that the stress and the fear culminated, erupted and I was crying uncontrollably in the boys' bathroom when Mr. Dixon found me. I was shaking and panting with snot running out of my nose. I don't know if he was sent in because someone reported me in there, but he took me to the teacher's lounge alone. I was still crying hard, heaving and hysterically. He kept asking me what is wrong, he couldn't understand why I was so upset. I couldn't even talk. Finally, I was able to tell him. He kept reassuring and trying to calm me that it was *"okay"* and *"not a big deal,"* but I wasn't crying about the lunch. I was scared that they would find out what went on in my house.

Mr. Dixon gave me his lunch and he told me to stay in the teacher's lounge until I felt ready to come out. I never forgot what he did to help me that day. Recently, I met Mr. Dixon for lunch and asked him if he remembered that day. I wanted to thank him and explain why I was so upset. Just after I began describing the incident, he interrupted me and said, *"I remember that, I think you were in fifth or sixth grade."* So, that day was significant and memorable to him too.

When I told my sister that I met with Mr. Dixon and why, she told me yet another account that I never knew of before. Immediately upon my completion she quickly responded. She coldly replied that when she, too, went to school without a lunch she *"went to the convent and the nuns gave (her) saltines..."*

There were times I went to school without wearing underwear, I am not certain why, if the wash wasn't done or some other reason. I remember opening my drawer and there would be nothing there. I knew that I was not going to say anything about it.

My neighbors, the Kent's, directly across the street were a husband-wife who were both Pittsburgh police officers and occasionally would babysit me in their home. I was afraid of them because of how my father spoke about police, but they were very nice to me. One day, when I was 6, my parents were talking about how Mr. Kent shot himself in the head with his service revolver in his house. I thought about that a lot. I didn't witness it, but I knew everything about it because my parents spoke in great detail about it in front of me.

I used to stare at the windows of their house and wondered what room he did it in. They had gold shag carpeting and their house was very clean and organized. They let me choose what to watch what I wanted on TV too. I would look over at that house and wonder, *"Did he do it on the shag carpeting?"* *"Did he have his policeman's uniform on?"*

Later a new family moved in their house. *"Did they know what happened in that house, their house?"*

I thought a lot about Mr. Kent and suicide, why would he do that? No one ever talked to me about it and there was no one who was going to talk to me.

I was told the story of how my cousin came home to find her mother, my Great Aunt Helen, dead, hanging in their kitchen. Her suicide was spoke about openly in my presence.

I knew that house well and every time we drove past that street I would think about that.

Depression is laced genetically throughout my family. My Grandmother breast fed the new born infants of her sister, Genevieve, and sister in law, Vera for the first months of their lives because of their "*melancholia*," then unknown elongated periods of severe post-partum depression. They would put a bed into their dining room where my Aunt Genevieve would stay for months after the births of her children. They just "*waited until she came out*" as my Grandmother explained it to me. My Uncle had depressive periods where he stayed in bed for days. Obviously, there was a genetic pathway in my family for severe issues and I tried to explain this to my father once. As I progressed he figured out what I was getting at and he exploded, "*there (was) nothing wrong with (him)! All that bullshit!*" According to him, everyone else had a "*problem*" but not him.

There were several alcoholics in my extended family, including two of my grandparents, and the effects of that caused many scandal-type tales. I heard too many of these stories and witnessed some. The adults of my family all played a card game called "*500*" that require four players and was like a watered-down version of Bridge. Many nights they would only have three players and they would make me play — this started when I was 10 years old. Often, they would get me out of bed to complete a game. Of course, I wanted to play, be with the grown-ups and stay up late, but I always had to be my father's partner in the game. This would often end with him yelling at me about how I played. The environment would be some of them drinking, talking, telling stories and as the alcohol took effect those stories became wide open, unfiltered, profane and "NC17."

That was me and that was my life.

One seemingly positive memory that I can think of about my father was when he would sometimes let me stay up and watch late night television, "*Movies till Dawn*," on a TV channel, WTOV from Steubenville, Ohio. It was mostly westerns, John Wayne, and so on. Gradually, this became very disturbing to me because somehow, I concluded that everyone in these films who got shot and died, all the cowboys and Indians who got killed were real people who wanted to commit suicide but didn't have the "guts" to do it themselves, so they just signed up to be in a movie and they were killed. I thought the killing was real, these people went somewhere and filmed these movies and where actually shot. I thought about this many times as a small boy and I never thought about asking my father about it. I remember lying on the floor watching these movies with him on the couch. If I did ask him, he might yell or make fun of me or not let me watch them anymore. Those movies became very scary to me, disturbing and disruptive.

I watched *"Deliverance"* with killings and men raping another man. I couldn't have been 12 years old. Why did all these people want to die? I never told or asked anyone that and I assume that somehow in time I realized that it wasn't true. I guess I never asked my mother because then she wouldn't let me stay up anymore. There were many things like that I kept to myself. It was safer that way. Sadly, I came up with my own explanations which made it more confusing for me.

As a child I wanted him to catch baseball with me and take me to a Pirate game like my friends' fathers did. When I was 30 years old I drove to his garage with two baseball gloves and I asked him to catch with me. I said, *"I don't want to have to say that I never caught baseball with my dad."* He did it for a few minutes, but now I realize that was my defense and coping mechanisms trying to make him, us, everything *"normal."* Maybe for those five minutes it was, in some distant way but you can never go back, but that was the best I had.

Throughout my life, I am consciously aware immediately if I see another family's photograph in a home or on a Christmas card. My attention and focus locks onto the image and the thoughts that follow of how nice that must have been for them. If you would be able to visit the house I grew up in you would discover that there were no displayed pictures of the four members of my family anywhere. No photographs of the four of us. No family vacation pictures, no holiday pictures, not one framed picture of us at all. None.

Chapter 8:

THE COMPANY HE KEPT

"You can tell a lot about someone by the friends he has"

MY FATHER SPENT ALMOST OF HIS TIME OUT in his garage in our backyard separate from the house. While the other boys were with their Dads who helped coach, or were picking their sons up from practice, he would send one of his hangers-on to drive me home. All of them were dependent on him in some way. He had control over them and he liked that. Some he loaned them their down payment on their houses, others he loaned them bail money or just he kept their cars running and on the road.

My Grandmother did not approve of these men some much so that she had it written in her will she did not want these people living in her house after she died. Several of these men were convicted felons and they spent their time hanging out or *"working"* with him in his garage. She didn't want them in her house, even after she was gone.

He built a large four car garage in the backyard. Later when the mill closed down he ran an illegal body shop back their full time. On any given day you might find all types of individuals hanging out for hours. One guy was an interstate cocaine trafficker, another one of his best friends from childhood who prostituted his own wife, a man who served jail time for raping his own child, while others had DUI's, were formally charged and convicted of domestic violence (one had a wife that looked like a very unsuccessful professional boxer, with her faced scarred from all the beatings), and yet another burned down a local bar because he did not like African-Americans in his neighborhood…I heard all the stories and I could go on and on. I knew these men and exactly what they did when I was just a 12-year-old child.

These characters were always hanging around our house, watching TV or in the garage. They all had very odd and colorful nicknames. Remember, everyone talked openly about everything in front of me. He would leave the child incest rapist in the garage while my sister was home alone – a mere 20 yards away. When I was in college I asked him if he was concerned about that, having a known pedophile so close to his own daughter? I don't remember getting any answer at all. I know I didn't like it.

Sometimes one of these men might have a prostitute waiting for them in their car parked in front of my house while they came back to his garage to pay him or talk to him. If you needed fireworks, jewelry, holiday flowers or any trendy item (mood rings, calculators, etc.) at the time one of them would probably have it available and sell it to you out of their trunk. All his *"friends"* brought their cars to be fixed, or sometimes just have an illegal inspection sticker applied by my father. One convicted felon and wife beater brought his car to my Dad once, and I was standing there when he pulled up. The *"car problem"* that he needed to be repaired? Bullet holes in the rear fender and trunk lid.

My father was also a *"hustler."* He hustled used cars, car parts, motor oil, tires, coupon books, anything he could get his hands on to make money. He stole from his employers incessantly, justifying like they **owed** him. He was always "wheeling and dealing," looking for an opportunity.

My father always told me what *"dirtbags"* the police were, how corrupt and unqualified they were. The exact opposite of what I was being taught at school. *"Thou shalt not steal,"* and if I *"had a problem to find and tell policeman.* He hated cops. One message that I received consistently was how *"bad"* the police were. How they enjoyed "catching" people, abused their power, were corrupt and *"on the take"* how any *"asshole on the unemployment line"* could do their job. He would rant about it up and down his emotional levels. Now, I can see that the message was clear and that I as a child was to avoid them at all costs. Today, I have several friends in several branches of law enforcement including our local magistrate and district attorney who are admirable people.

Once a guy owed my father money, most of the people around owed him money, and he liked that, having everyone dependent on him. This also explains the people he kept around him. Well, this guy couldn't pay what he owed so he asked my father if we *"had cable television?"* Next thing that occurred, this man went to his trunk, attached climbing spikes to his boots and climbed up the telephone pole in front of our house. We had cable and several pay stations for the next three years. Another man paid him with a paper bag full of food stamps. My father gave the bag to my mother who immediately complained she would not use them. My mother was too embarrassed to use herself because she didn't want to be seen in public using food stamps. I saw lots of cash in many amounts in tool boxes and once I saw a paper bag in his truck with $25,000 in it.

One day, a man came to his garage for the first time and as they were talking about some business. Changing the subject, the man asked him about one of his cars, *"Is that for sale?"* My father looked at him very seriously and responded, *"Everything you see here is for sale...., including **him!**"* and he pointed at me. I told that story many times and laughed as if it was a joke, but how it made me feel was just the opposite to me.

When our son was born, my father said that he would be very bright because my wife is *"very intelligent"* and I was *"not an idiot."* Again, I would repeat this tale over and over as a punch line, but that is yet another example how he repeatedly degraded me in public.

My father felt since he ***"provided"*** for his *family,* that he fulfilled his entire role and met all his responsibilities. Now, I know that his *"hustle"* didn't stop when he came in the house. He hustled us, manipulated us into his needs and whims, his mood swings and his demands. Nothing else mattered, not to him. Any issues we had and schedules or places we needed to go was always a major problem for him. He only cared about himself, not my mother and definitely not me or my sister.

I felt that I was living in a potential life-threatening situation with no chance of escape. I couldn't run away or pray it away. I had passive suicidal and homicidal ideations, but I never planned or acted on it. I just cried and was always afraid. I did this as a young boy in my room. Thinking how much I could hurt him by hurting me.

He told me stories about cars falling off jacks and killing mechanics he knew, and I would hope that would happen to him. Then I would feel so horrible that I had these ideas in my head. As I got older I became very reckless on my bicycle, climbing trees higher than everyone else, skiing the steepest hills, going further out in the ocean than anyone else, volunteering to box guys I knew were much better than me, etc. In college I worked parking cars in a high rise building downtown. I had keys to the elevators and would go up to the roof and walk right up to the edge, 27 floors down. I would never do any of those things today.

Recently, I read an analogy that I used to try to explain how it felt to a friend: *"It's like driving with one foot on the gas and one on the brake all the time. I had no idea what was going happen at any time."* We were all there waiting to be interrogated or until he found something he could attack, then he would take it to the worst level he possibly could. He would walk in and I would freeze, he would change the TV channel, if you were in the bathroom you got out as fast as possible, just try to predict where or what he might focus on.

Chapter 9:

THE "GRANDFATHER"

"Why does Grandpap say such mean things about Grandma?"

LATER, WHEN I HAD CHILDREN I TRIED TO include him in the things that I did that I has hoped for as a child. I took him on trips and to events, on a birthday trip to Gettysburg for my son with his friends, museums, a Pirate game, and more. He would sabotage so many of these and make them extremely uncomfortable — his behavior and antics were impossible to ignore.

In the summer I take my kids on "surprise days". These are day trips that I plan where I try to find interesting activities and destinations for them. They have no idea where we are going. Once, on one of these trips, I took my children to a nice restaurant for lunch and we invited him with us. When my son was young, he liked places with balconies and decks, so we were at a restaurant over-looking the city. It was really nice and a special time. My father decided the menu was too expensive. I always paid for everything and picked up every check, but he refused to order anyhow. He said it was too expensive, complained and sulked. We tried to ignore it and enjoy the experience, but he would have none of that. He continued to rant and complain about the prices. Afterwards, my mother would thank me for taking him and rave about how happy he is when he comes home making me think

I was helping her by suffering through these painful and embarrassing occasions in order to somehow improve <u>her</u> life. She was manipulating me to continue with this emotionally abusive *"family tradition."*

Today, when I see children with their grandparents in public, I feel sad for my children. I know that is out of my control and it is my parent's conscious choice not to be involved, but it still a produces a disappointment for me.

Chapter 10:

MOTHER

"You know Jimmy, your mother will never leave him...."

MY FAMILY VARIED IN THE METHODS WE USED to deal with the environment we were in. Our defense and coping mechanisms were unconsciously challenged. Sporadically there might have been small successes but we all suffered. My mother normalized and rationalized his abuse, behavior and violence and she continues to do so to this day. Now as an adult, I continue to recall and process so many examples of her false hopes, fictitious preventions and planned avoidances. I participated knowingly in some while others, I was manipulated into by her consciously and/ or unconsciously. My attempts to confront her about this issue was immediately dressed down as: *"It wasn't THAT bad, you exaggerate, you had it good"* or *"He was never around much anyhow,"* *"Oh, Jimmy he was never home!"* These statements hurt me, and I didn't understand why. She was invalidating my experiences, my life, my pain and that was her submissive and apathetic style of manipulation and abuse.

My parents bought their first new car – a 1972 Impala. I remember sitting in the front seat of that car, so I know that I was six years old. It was summer, which would be my birthday. The Chevy Impala was dark blue with a vinyl roof, dark blue interior and had one long bench seat in the front.

By this point in my life, I had witnessed my father hitting my mother, threatening her, swearing and screaming multiple times. On this particular day, just my mother and I were leaving my aunt and uncle's house. My defenses were down, my father was still in the house, and I remember her being upset at that immediate time. They had a fight and we were leaving without him.

I vividly remember where that Chevy Impala was parked that night, on the right side of the street along the high curb. The doors were long and really heavy. I remember sitting there on the front seat when the car doors closed, my mother's demeanor changed. That was not unusual, in public we always had to keep up the appearance and preserve the secret. Before we pulled away my mom looked down at me and her face was crying and puffy. She said, "*You know that your uncle hits your aunt too?*" Then she put the car in drive and we silently drove away. She never clarified her statement. I just looked straight ahead. I remember immediate numbness, I remember being cold, scared and I think right then I knew that I had nothing more to hope for because my life was never going to change. I knew that my "*secret*" was never going be over.

How does an adult say that to a little boy? My mother's life must have been in so much turmoil and denial that she went to that level to justify her codependence to a small boy. I guess for her that divorce was not an option in our lower middle class, Catholic lives. She didn't have the money; the embarrassment and public pressure would have been extreme. She was stuck and so was I, but she had a choice.

Many times, I thought about that, imagining my uncle hitting my aunt. For years I thought about that trying to imagine it, where it happened and why. I would be in their house for holidays and look around and wonder about how it happened, what may have been said, etc.

My mother told me once that she was called to appear at my grade school, high school and college to have meetings about me. This was another thing that we joked about. I always assumed that it was due to me arguing with teachers over religion, abortion, and other issues. Once I threw my baseball glove at my gym teacher because I was mad at a call he made during a pick-up softball game. I just assumed that the meetings were over "discipline" type things. Now, I realize teachers must have been assessing that there was something indicating that they might need to investigate my "*home life.*" Why else were they calling? I never had any academic issues…

My mother was asked to meet with the dean of my school during my undergraduate college experience. She was never clear on why or what was said. I pushed her on this once. She said the dean asked her to describe my "*relationship with (my) father.*" My mother claims that she said that was "*none of her business*" and left. I will never know the truth, but I do know that she was summoned to have a meeting with my dean while I was in college and that my father was a subject that was addressed.

A stray dog violently attacked me when I was 4 years old. I was playing outside in the summertime. The dog dragged me from the tiny tricycle I was riding and ripped the back of my thigh open. I was bleeding, lying on the sidewalk a few houses up from my Grandmother's house. A few teenagers carried me back there. I remember going to the emergency room and since it was a stray dog, I had received six rabies shots in my abdomen and thighs. Upon my discharge I stayed at my Grandmother's house. My legs and stomach hurt so bad from the injections, I was totally stiff and cramped, I couldn't walk. I was so scared — I'm still afraid of strange dogs, the sounds of leashes, barking…

As an adult and parent, I asked my mother about that day since I was curious about the actual incident. I wanted to know who carried me home. She told me that she "*didn't remember*" and "*that it was so long ago.*" That answer was beyond comprehension to me — if my child was bleeding from a dog attack and had to be treated at a hospital including rabies shots, that memory would be ingrained in me. Did I mean so little to her that she didn't remember? Or was it like so many other unpleasant memories that she just "forgot" it?

My mother would try to create a "home" type of environment when my father was gone. She would try to make up for it with little toys, special events, restaurants just the two of us, but we always kept quiet, always kept the secret so no one would know what really went on in our house. When my father worked the 3-11 evening shift my mother and I did have nice times watching T.V. together and making popcorn at night. We would share the couch, drink Pepsi, I would brush her hair and she would let me stay up late — things that my friends weren't allowed to do. I would value those times, but at the same time I would be sad because I knew it was temporary, episodic at best. I felt like I was helping her and protecting her in a way and that made me feel good.

I spent long periods trying to understand why it couldn't be "like that all the time." I created all kinds of theories and hypotheses about how my life became the way it did. My parents talked and argued about all subjects in front of me. Just like I was invisible, or I was a piece of furniture. They spoke of adult subjects and family matters, argued over money issues, everything right in front of me. I knew about affairs and cheating, wife swapping, relatives who were sexually abused, etc. These items were woven through the nasty threats and profanity laced insults they threw around at each other. *"I hate you!" "You Bitch!" "Drop dead Bitch!"* and on and on.

Once when I was very young, seven or eight, the older boys in my neighborhood showed me a Playboy magazine they had hidden in the woods. I knew that this was wrong. I was scared. I didn't know what to do. This weighed on me. Days later, we left for a "vacation," an unplanned drive to Wildwood, NJ or Ocean City, MD. My parents never, ever made any motel reservations. This resulted every time with driving in and out of motel parking lots with "no vacancy" and my father getting angrier and angrier. I could never understand why we through the same routine over and over.

She wanted a pool and he wanted cheap and the war broke open on a new front with the body count in the backseat.

On this occasion, we were driving on the turnpike and I was so frightened and stressed because I was going to tell my parents what I saw in the woods with the older boys. I was going to communicate my fears and share my feelings with them, so they could console me and support me and care for me. I thought about this for miles and miles: I attempted to verbalize and to express this terrible and confusing thing. I can vividly remember this. Many times, I almost said it, the words almost came out of my mouth. I was so scared. What happened next was a microcosm of my childhood. An argument between them led to a fight which led to screaming and swearing, this culminated with my father throwing my mother's 8-Track tapes out the window all over the Pennsylvania Turnpike as he drove, threats and silence followed.

I never ever came close to trusting them again. I never shared that problem or any other issue that I had. I was alone in that backseat of that Chevy Impala driving down the Pennsylvania Turnpike in the summer going to the beach. I could never trust anyone at all. Somewhere there were tapes of Art Garfunkel, Anne Murray and Bread shattered all over the highway. Broken up just like me.

He would make fun of my mother, but I didn't always understand the "*jokes.*" One line he would repeatedly say, and laugh was "*Big bum Betty, with a big bum and little plums.*" I didn't understand what that meant, how hurtful and mean that was. I could not comprehend why he thought it was funny, but I do remember the sadness and hurt on my mother's face and that she did nothing about it all. She would just take it, every time.

He was extremely misogynistic, and when I was alone with him, he spoke about other women like I was an adult. That was upsetting to me. He would look at them and tell me to do it too. Make comments and inappropriate remarks about them. He would continue this years later with my sister who is unmarried. He would say directly to her how she wears *"lesbian shoes"* or things like he *"doesn't know what the hell is wrong with (her),"* she *"is a bitch just like her mother,"* and that he *"feels sorry for the poor son of a bitch that ends up with her."* I don't know how much of these rants that my sister had to endure alone.

Later, I would learn why it was so easy for him to be so mean to her. My mother was a "worker," a volunteer, an organizer. She worked full time in an office, was President of my Catholic grade school PTA, she worked the bingo and all the candy sales. She even used to work on Sundays at the concession stands at Three Rivers Stadium for the Steeler games. I don't know how much we needed the money or if she just needed excuses to get away from him. Either of these possibilities was admirable to me then, but not at all to me today.

She left me alone with him.

She attended all my little league games, my events and practices. In 1979, she took me to the National League Championship series and to a World Series game, just the two of us. That was a great memory but like everything, we always had to be concerned when we came home. I am very thankful for that but sad too. Those were experiences that a boy was supposed to do with his father, his *"Dad."*

She could make me feel better sometimes but others were puzzling to me. She used to say to me many times, *"You should have been a girl, you have such pretty hair."* She would say that in public too. Did she want a girl more than me? I found this very confusing and never understood that–I still don't.

I remember once when a man approached her at a concession stand at Three Rivers Stadium, and I assume appropriately *"made a pass"* at her by asking her out. I vividly remember this as I was standing on the other side. Her response was, *"I am sorry, but I am a happily married woman."* I knew that was totally untrue. I knew lying was wrong. I wondered why she would say something that I knew, unfortunately way too well, that was an absolute lie. Then I thought and created an imaginary world of how the man might be a great guy and maybe we could leave with him that he would take us away. I thought he might be like one of the Dads on TV and how nice that would be.

Later, I have discovered that my mother was the child and grandchild of extremely abusive alcoholics. These environments were her *"normal."* I have come to understand that she thrives in the eternal victim role. She tells herself that *"the secret"* is unknown to everyone while at the same time achieving a level of satisfaction and comfort that she is and always has been the victim of these people. Once I told her that she just *"replaced one abuser with another,"* and she just looked at me in silence.

Once I asked my mother if she knew if my father was abused as a child. She looked at me astonished and just said *"No."* In some demented way that must work for her, but my sister and I paid for it. She lives a generational cycle of victimization and abuse, but she is not innocent. She had choice and her children desperately needed care and protection. Her manipulation of me had – and still has–no beginning and no end. I am still identifying and realizing incidents of this.

I have maintained all of the gravesites my great-grandparents, grandparents and military members of my family for all my adult life. Once when while I was still trying to maintain a relationship with her and not with my father, my mother suggested that I stop taking care of my paternal Grandmother's gravesite. Why? Because it made my father angry that I was doing it. This would then make her life easier. Selfish? I don't know. I don't care. He never maintained her grave. I still plant flowers there every year.

Now her situation, her role and participation in our abusive environment has become exposed. When I started this process of the truth, the therapy and throughout my questions and her answers, my mother attempted to make it appear that she was supportive, but she was just circling the wagons to protect herself and *"the secrets."*

My mother called and invited a former high school student of mine to "dinner." This individual babysat my children is now a close friend of my family. This person was young and impressionable. She was 20 years old and my mother planned to groom her just like any predator would. She lured her into a *"dinner"* only to instruct her not to *"believe me"* and explain that I was *"lying," "making all these stories up,"* and *"exaggerating,"* these abuses and making it sound like it was worse.

A few days later, this young woman called me and said she needed to talk with me. She appeared at my house crying and extremely upset. She was afraid that I was going to be mad at her. Finally, she told me what my mother said and attempted to do. I successfully identified this as another example of my mother's manipulative practice to rationalize her acceptance of that life and sadly attempt to protect the *secrets*.

Another example was when my children were younger, and we drove to my parents' house to pick her up. We were going to "take Grandma" to dinner with us and to see a famous comedian downtown. My children were all smiles ready for the big day. As my mother walked down her sidewalk — which was about 20 yards long — the front door quickly swung open and my father screamed across the whole neighborhood, *"YEAH, YOU GO! DON'T' COME BACK YOU BITCH! YOU HEAR ME!!! DON'T COME BACK HERE YOU BITCH!!!"*

Now, as shocking as that is, what occurred next after she got in the car with us is a microcosm of my whole life. Nothing. Absolutely nothing was said, not addressed or explained, we just acted like nothing happened at all. We went to dinner and all acted like nothing at all happened. I didn't realize it, but I was modeling the acceptance of the abusive behavior for my children just like my parents did to me all my life.

My wife and I bought our first house in a very nice suburb and we really were excited to set up our "home."

We planted a garden, painted the nursery and had our son a year later. It was exciting, and we were busy adapting to this new married, parenting lifestyle. One evening that I vividly remember explains the two worlds I was unknowingly living in. We were in bed and it was very late. Our son was in the next room sleeping and the phone rang. It was my mother. Her voice was pressured and serious, *"Jimmy, I need you to do something. I need you to go to Stiffy's in McKees Rocks."* I lived in the South Hills, an area of beautiful lawns, parks and quiet and calm. "McKees Rocks" is a rough area just west on the edge of Pittsburgh, not the place to be at night. *"Stiffy's"* is as exactly as it sounds, a low-level strip joint with plywood walls and travel posters scattered throughout. Often the site of newspaper stories of crimes and related activities. So, here is my supposedly Catholic mother calling me to leave my family, drive into a dangerous area, alone, to go into a known nuisance "gentleman's club."

"WHAT?! Where do you want me to go?" I shockingly responded.

"Jimmy, I need you to go down there," she repeated.

"WHY? What? Wait, what do you want me to do?" I still couldn't comprehend what she was asking me to do.

My mother finally got to her point, *"Your cousin is dancing in there. I need you to go down there and get her out of there!"* she declared.

"You want me to drive down into the Rocks and walk in there? What am I supposed to do? Tackle her and drag her out? Are you serious?"

She was.

I hung up the phone, and my wife was looking at me, puzzled over what she just heard. How was I supposed to explain this to her? That this is the family she married in to?

Of course, I did not go. Why was my mother going to risk my safety, have me leave my wife and infant home alone in the middle of the night and drive alone into a high crime area?

Why? Because she would be embarrassed if anyone found out her niece was identified as exactly what she was. Why didn't she call her brother, the girl's father? I am sure she did, and either he didn't care, or she didn't want to risk what he might do.

I guess I was just expendable...

In 2015, I was nominated by one of my students for the **Pennsylvania State Teacher of the Year** and upon completion of the interviewing process I was named a finalist. This was a major honor and event, an event where my family, and the family of the student who nominated me where given a trip to "*Chocolate World*", Hershey, PA for a three-day program and ceremony. I also was permitted to choose a mentor and representative from the school district and his wife to join us.

This was an unbelievable time for me, to be nominated by a student and to successfully progress through a year-long process of multiple levels of essays, videos and interviews. This was a culmination of my entire career as an educator. The planning and excitement all came crashing down the evening before we were due to leave.

My mother was going to join us for the trip. I honestly can't remember who called me first. Her brother, my uncle, explained to me that my father had taken my mother's car keys and physically blocked her car with his, not letting her leave the house. He was threatening to kill her and himself and my mother was locked in her bedroom.

My luggage was packed for this great honor that I would be receiving with speeches by me and about me. Now, I had to deal with this.

Now I had to drive to their house and get my mother out of there that night, so we could all leave the next morning to attend my special event. That whole weekend I listened to speeches and watched as other honorees introduce their fathers and describe how influential their fathers were in their lives.

I was introduced to some of them, I put on the fake smile like I was trained to my whole life. I went through the motions, tried to act "normal." I tried to enjoy it, but I was right back where I started. He won, he was in control, he ruined my weekend and all I thought about was him.

Why I couldn't please him and why was he always so mean to me?

Through therapy and endless hours revisiting my entire life, I now understand and am thoroughly amazed how this situation was a representation of my entire life. If at any time the attention was not on my father or he had to do something that he was not going to be the focus of, he would sabotage it to whatever level he had to, up to and including violence, in order make everyone more miserable than himself. He had an arsenal of skills and meanness and would take it to any level to accomplish his sick and destructive needs. I have created timelines of banquets, games, school functions, events, holidays, etc. that he would destroy for me or all of us. I hated every minute of public events that we had to go to because I felt that every single person there knew the hell I had to go through, screaming, swearing, threatening all the way there and then the fake smiles that went on as soon as the car doors opened.

When my family and my mother returned from the **Teacher of the Year Awards** event in Hershey, I had to go back to his house to take her home. When we returned from Hershey from that weekend I had a new final challenge waiting for me.

When I began this introspective process of my life, I started to contact neighbors, teachers, coaches, friends who knew my family when I was a child. This was frightening to me because I was afraid of what I might find out. Julie was a close friend of my mother's and our neighbor who lived across the street. She told me–30 years later from when I grew up–*"Jimmy, you have to understand. Your father was a very unhappy man; he never showed affection of any kind. He has no respect for women and was extremely bitter and mean, and, you know…you know that your Mom will never leave him…"*

Chapter 11:

THE "SECRET"

"I always felt like I had one hundred secrets and one thousand lies…"

I CANNOT CLEARLY RECALL THE SPECIFIC events in their entirety; my sister remembers much more than me, the details and the quotes. I spent to so much time and energy forgetting or effort in modifying somehow to make it manageable, tolerable. My sister was born when I was 6 years old. I clearly remember what occurred before that. I saw him beat my mother physically. That was hard for me to type, it's hard for me to read right now. I witnessed that, how many times, I am not certain. Too many times, I often get sad for that little boy whose innocence was coldly sacrificed by my father's weakness and cowardice. Some I witnessed and, some I heard, but I know that I cried about them all. I went to school, baseball practice or to a friend's house so many times with red puffy eyes I started to believe that people didn't notice.

I have one very specific memory still is alarming to me to this day. I do not remember consciously deciding or thinking about what I did but I can recall the aftermath.

I was playing in the living room on a nice sunny day. There were no problems at that time. I had no predetermined idea of about was to take place. My father came up the stairs from the basement and stood facing the living room from the archway. Quickly I ran up and punched him square in the penis as hard as I could. He dropped to the floor screaming at me. I ran up the stairs as fast as I could and darted under my bed deep into the corner abutted along the walls.

He violently and loudly thrashed up the stairs screaming and swearing as he dropped to the floor of my bedroom. He was reaching and swinging at me under my bed, but I was just out of his reach. My mother verbally tried to stop him and gradually he did, but then he just laid on my bedroom floor right on the edge of my bed. I couldn't get out if I wanted to and I certainly didn't want to. I was terrified. He was laying just outside my bed like a monster. I don't know how long I stayed under there. What would possess a child to do that? Just like everything that happened in that house, it was never spoke of again. My mother never came to comfort me after he left my room, either.

I wanted my mother to leave and take us away, to "break up" our family but at the exact same time I wanted to "protect" our family and keep it from breaking up. It was a merry-go-round that never ended. It was paralyzing emotionally, a fantasy that someday it would all be normal, and we could forget all the ugliness. Again, this is actually upsetting me right now just writing this.

I was sent to Catholic school; most of my grandparents were church goers. My living grandparents were devout in church attendance, the sacraments and said their rosaries every day before their soap operas. My mother would take us to church sometimes, my father would never go.

I was an altar boy from ages 9-14 and I tried to pay attention, to have faith, to listen to the nuns in class talk about goodness and compassion. I never had any faith ever, not one time. People will say *"don't lose your faith."* I have no idea what that means. I never had any faith, all my time in all those masses I attended and all the services where I was an altar boy I just thought about one idea. *"Why? Where is God for me? Why did He let me have to live like I did? Why wouldn't He come for me and protect me? Punish my father? Reward my Mom?"*

When I was in the first grade a nun had a breakdown and lost total control in class. She was screaming and yelling, throwing books and dumping desks. We were all crying. I remember the names of my classmates and where we were sitting. One girl kept crying as the nun screamed at her to stop and in one quick, sudden movement the nun ripped a handful of her hair out of her head. Finally, a teacher from across the hall came over and gradually the nun was removed from our classroom and we never saw her again. I don't remember any discussions or explanations, but I do remember that girl came back to school with her hair combed in a way to cover up the damage. This nun represented the church? I was in first grade. I was paddled by nuns violently that was way beyond a "punishment."

I never believed, and I never trusted any of it. There was no God for me. The idea of the "Catholic Guilt" was so real to me. *What did I do to be mistreated so much?* I must be bad. I must have sinned so horribly in the eyes of God that this was my punishment. The Catholic religion has no place to help someone like me; just the opposite.

As I got older I became angrier. The church failed me, as did all of the adults in my family and I had nowhere to go. I was just an angry kid hoping and wishing for something I still thought was possible. Then I became an angrier young man...

When I was 14 he hit her again. (Probably many more times too but it is just very difficult for me to recall the specific events.) This time, it was in the dining room and it was daylight. I don't know the reason, there was no consistency to why or when. He wasn't a drinker, there was no precursor or stereotypical trigger that caused him to abuse her, my sister or me. There would be long periods of weeks, sometimes months without an incident but I always knew what was just under the surface.

This time I stepped between them, there was a lot of yelling and screaming, crying and threats. He didn't hit her anymore that night and he didn't hit me that time either. The clear memory I do have is crying with my mom and telling her it would be different when I was bigger, when I was older. I promised that I wouldn't let him do that anymore and that I could stop him. She would make excuses for him, *"Jimmy you don't understand. He has to work."* or *"He doesn't understand, he is sick"* or *"He won't be around for a while now…it will be ok."*

Our mother perfected the idea in us that we should worry about her. That she was the victim and we need to support her. My sister and I can see now this theme throughout our lives. We were always worried about her. **Her** safety, how **she** feels, **her** stress, how we could help **her**. Later, she would call me crying, *"I don't know what to do,"* but when I would call her in a similar fashion she would tell me *"Deal with it, put it all away and forget about it,"* and *"Stop feeling sorry for yourself."* There was always a very small window for me and I was expected to handle all of it and move on. I was trying to rescue a *"family"* that never existed. I kept the abuse a secret from myself too. The aftermath is always etched into my mind more than the abuse itself.

Chapter 12:

REALIZATION

"We had no one to protect us and no one was coming for us..."

WHEN MY FATHER WAS GONE, MY MOTHER made me feel special and I aligned myself to her. I put all of my hopes in her. Everything, I was totally dependent emotionally on her. She and I went to the mall and I saw an advertisement for a baseball competition, "Pitch, Hit and Run." Now, my actual baseball ability did not come close to my dreams, but when I saw that big placard I blurted out that I wanted to enter. Never would I put myself at risk to ask for something like that from my father, but I felt safe to expose myself like this with my mom. Her reaction? *"Why would you want to do that? You won't win."* That hurt so bad, I never thought she would be like him too. It was crushing, I felt totally alone. I was 11 years old.

She repeated this behavior throughout my life, but her involvement and reactions were beginning to become less important to me. Today, that part of me has been amputated and any feelings left are just numb. I did enter the competition and finished second overall. I still have the plaque won too but it has nothing to do with baseball to me. I had to believe in myself. Looking back, I guess that I was realizing that I was on my own in more ways than I even knew.

When I was 13 years old, on a very pleasant spring day my mother told my sister and I to *"pack."* As often the case, my sister remembers more of this than I do. It was in the afternoon and I remember running out of the house carrying the little portable television set I received as Christmas present that year.

Now, I did not ask for a TV, never thought of anything expensive like that. There was always only one television in our house. He watched it. He controlled it and it was not pleasant being in the room as he watched **"his"** TV. My mother was not allowed to have one, so the small television was my *"present"* that year. It was white. I carried it out to her car as quickly as I could with a bag of my clothes.

We drove away and went to my grandparent's house. My mother "left" my father, more like *escaped.* I think we were there for three days. I really don't remember any specifics about it. I don't remember where I slept, if I went to school — nothing like that. What I do remember is everything that was done before had one objective, to keep up the appearance of a normal family and protect the *"secret."* Now, the opposite had occurred.

People were now going to know, but I was too young to understand that everyone already knew. I really can't remember what I did. A family summit resulted from this. Everyone in one room. My grandparents, my aunts and uncles all together in a very quiet and serious meeting I was so embarrassed and sad. My aunt asked me in front of this entire gathering what I wanted to do. I was terrified and forced to speak. I have no idea what I said but all I thought about is, *"What he was going to do to me now if we were going to go back?"*

I could barely breathe, I was horrified. I didn't say anything. Our whole existence was in his hands, my identity, my self-esteem was all controlled by him. This was worse than that. My Aunt then asked him what he wanted. He mumbled, *"I want my family back,"* while holding his head in his hands. The kids were told to *"go out and play."* I don't know what was said after that. I just kept thinking the same thought. He was going to kill her and maybe all of us for this. I was convinced of that.

Three days after we left, we went back. I don't remember what is was like. Nothing stands out, so I assume that is was a short attempt at good behavior on his part, but it didn't last. I have no memory of hope that it was going to be any different and I know that it wasn't. Same issues, same fears, same fights, same yelling, all the same. No improvement, no change, no difference.

The first time I went to therapy, I was still in graduate school. I wasn't totally truthful, and I kept my *"secret"* from our discussions. I never told anyone about my abuse history.

I kept having a reoccurring dream at the time. I called it the *"Alligator Dream."* Many nights I would have the same vision which was very similar and disturbing to me. My house as a child had a homemade bathroom directly underneath the stairs in the unfinished basement. A small "room" was created by closing in the area underneath the stair case. The floor was exposed concrete, walls were bare cinder block and it was very scary to me when I was little. I hated and rarely ever went in there. No sink, small and dark, it was the bathroom he and his friends used when they worked in his garage. It was very similar to a public gas station bathroom in smell and lighting. One small light bulb, cold and damp. I have heard of these since being referred to as *"a Pittsburgh bathroom."*

In my dream, my father and I were both crammed in this "bathroom" which was barely large enough for one person aside from two grown men. I was in my twenties in the dream and in real life. The door was slightly ajar and there were several violent alligators attacking us trying to get in. My father had a broom stick in one hand that he used to fight the alligators and was trying to keep the door closed by pulling the door by the knob with the other hand at the same time. I just stood behind him doing nothing. The alligators were biting, growling and gnashing their teeth at us violently. I was very upset and alarmed by the thought of this.

Many nights resulted in the same dream and identical feelings of me analyzing it and staying awake. I addressed it in therapy and was asked what I thought the meaning of it was many times. Of course, my immediate conclusion was that my father was *"taking care of my problems,"* that I *"wasn't responsible,"* that I *"wasn't a man,"* and so forth. The favorite tag line of my father's verbal abuse to me which I pelted with countless times was, **"YOU'LL NEVER BE A MAN!!!"** So that resonated in me over and over in my interpretation.

After a few sessions of me repeating my theories of how much of a failure and how "soft" I was, my therapist asked me a simple question. *"How do you know that the alligators weren't after <u>him</u>? That they weren't <u>his</u> alligators?"*

That question was the first step, the first glimmer of the idea that <u>he had the problem</u>, that <u>he was responsible</u>, and that I just might be innocent and <u>separate from him</u>.

Chapter 13:

THE E.R.

"I combined all these events in my head into one and
just put it away..."

I HAVE KEPT SECRETS MY WHOLE LIFE — MANY
I thought were to protect my sister. I honestly thought if I
didn't tell her she wouldn't know. Sounds obvious. More like
oblivious. I have found out after I began this process that my
sister remembers more and witnessed more of the incidents
that I tried to keep secret from her than I ever realized.

After we broke the silence, my sister and I started to discuss the events of our upbringing, I began to explain a secret
that I kept. One specific incident that I kept hidden away
was very fragmented in my mind. After many discussions
and phone calls, I finally decided to talk to my sister about it.

One time <u>before</u> my sister was born my father assaulted
my mother and cut her to the point where she had to go
to the hospital emergency room. Seconds after I fragilely
began to address this my sister interrupted me, *"Jimmy, I*
was there. I was 10. I went to the E.R. with them then they took
me to my friend's birthday party. They told me not to talk about it
and dropped me off at the birthday party."

I was speechless and stunned. How could my younger
sister know what I was talking about? She was not born
when that happened. Suddenly it struck me. It must have
happened more than once. My sister knew it the whole time

and she witnessed my father physically attack our mother. She knew more details and specifics than I did, and she kept her secret just like me all these years. But I knew I was very young when I saw the physical abuse so if she was 10 years old then I was 16. Was I so off in my memories or did it happen **twice**? How many times **could** it have happened? How many times **did** it happen?

The discussion continued. I can remember the house she went to. I know where it is right now because my parents made me go pick her up. The *"birthday party"* was a sleep over party but the girl's mother called and said that my sister was upset and wanted to come home, she did not want to sleep over. My parents knew why she was upset, did they go get her? Were they worried about her crying alone at this house? No, they sent me. I drove to the house and picked her up at 11:00 p.m. but I had no idea why my sister was so upset. Not until we had that discussion did I know.

Chapter 14:

RUNNING AWAY

"I felt like an emotional time bomb"

I NEVER ACTUALLY *"RAN AWAY"* I JUST escaped or got away as best I could. When I was very young, and they were screaming and fighting, sometimes I would just run out of my house to the top of the street and stand there. Today, I wonder what my neighbors thought of me just standing in the street a few hundred yards from my house crying at 7 a.m.

I remember once running out the front door early in the morning before school. I can't remember the exact event that caused me to run, but there was a lot of screaming. I know I was scared; I didn't want to see him scream at her again, swear at her again, hit her again. A few minutes past, and my Mom picked me up on the street and drove me to school. I should have been taken to a counselor and my mother to a battered women's shelter. I went to school feeling like that many times. Red puffy face and watered red eyes.

As I got older, I would run to my Aunt's house and stay there for hours, for dinner and many times overnight. No one, not my parents or extended family, ever asked why I was always there. I felt horrible that my little sister was left behind, but I was too young to do anything about that. I just had to get away for myself. Little did I know she would go on to witness more than I ever realized. Maybe even more than me.

There was a new family who moved into our neighborhood, across the street from my house after my sister was born. Their children were all older than me, teen-agers, who became my babysitters and later friends. Mr. and Mrs. Knight became great friends and extremely supportive of me. Their family was very different from any that I ever experienced in my short life. They yelled and fought, argued, but they didn't hide anything, they weren't ashamed, and they had no "*secret.*" They were all close, and their feelings good and bad, were right out in the open. They loved and cared for each other through everything. I felt hope in their house. Maybe I wasn't as damaged as I thought.

Slowly over the years, we would spend holidays there, they would babysit me and give me rides to practices. Mrs. Knight let my friends and me play in their yard while looked out for me. She always smiled when she saw me and made me feel special.

Mr. Knight was a WWII veteran, very relaxed and liked to have his Iron City beer, but he was a very happy drinker. I would watch sports events with him, do my homework at his house and–he would make me milkshakes and listen to me. I wasn't allowed to watch sports in my house. There was only one television in the house and my father didn't like any sports, so I couldn't watch. This was the 1970s and Monday Night Baseball and the NBC Game of the Week were the only two chances to see the rest of the Major League teams and American Leaguers play. One Sunday I was watching the Yankees versus the Red Sox. I loved Carlton Fisk, Jim Rice and Freddie Lynn, and I hated the Yankees. My father walked in, turned it off and yelled at me, called me "*lazy*" and worse. He said there was no reason to watch it at all since the Pirates weren't even playing. I could go to Mr. White's house and he would watch it with me. We watched Larry Bird and Magic, Kareem and the Lakers, John Havilcek and the Celtics and Al McGuire and his 1977 Marquette team.

Even before I entered my teens, the Knight's did something else for me, something that I never realized how special and caring it was until very recently. They purposely left their basement door unlocked for me around the clock, every day. Our neighborhood was a nicer one for being within the city limits, but crime was a real issue. I cannot estimate how times I went there, how many hours I spent there — many times alone. That was an oasis for me, a safety zone that I could control, and I am so thankful for that now. I am so fortunate that they trusted me like that. That door was never locked once. I reconnected with Mr. Knight's daughters recently, and they have been a tremendous resource for me in searching my past and an unyielding support for me. Their daughter, Natalie, who was at my house consistently through my childhood, told me this. *"Jimmy, do you know how many nights I heard my father get out of bed to go down stairs to make sure the basement door was UNLOCKED? He loved you."*

My Aunt gave me a small wrapped present for Christmas when I was 14. A gift in a jewelry type box. I opened it and it was a single red key on a white plastic keychain. She gave me a key to their house. She was consciously providing an escape for me, but at the same time, I didn't understand the reason why then. She obviously knew there was a problem in my life but that is far as she would go to help me.

Once my aunt told me a story about when I was very young. She said that she and my uncle were lying on the sofa together holding each other. She said I walked up near them and just stood there. I stared at them, standing in front of them. I had no memory of this at the time. When she told me this story I remembered it, and I do today as well. She asked me if I needed something, and I said *"no,"* but kept on staring. She asked me if I was okay and I responded, *"My parents never do that,"* and I ran away.

I never remembered that until she told me that story as an adult.

My football coach in high school, Dennis Wayne, had four children and coincidently used to be neighbors with the Knight family before they moved onto our street. My coach had a small addition on the back of their house with a television and large sofas. He too left that door unlocked and let me use that anytime I wanted. I went there many times. A few doors down from their house was the family of Mr. Costello, who was a teacher at my high school. Later, in my life they also left their door open for me. I spent many mornings and nights at their houses. Often, I went there when they were not home, watching TV or sleeping on their couches but mostly being away or getting away from my house. I am not sure if I searched these relationships out subconsciously or they saw through my façade. Maybe they had so much experience dealing with kids they were actively helping me. Probably a combination of these possibilities led them to help me. I am still realizing how kind and caring they were and continue to be for me and my family.

Today, I can see that I was not very good at keeping "*the secret.*" Doors were open for me to escape and hide, but that was the most anyone would or could do for me. I know it was the 1970s, therapy and family services were not as prevalent as today, nor would they be acceptable by my parents if they were. People stayed out of each other's business or just looked the other way. People did not reach out and intervene even when is was perceived to be so bad that people left the doors open. There was no internet, no "*Oprah,* no P.S.A.'s and no hotlines.

Chapter 15:

BREAKING POINT

"I was never as strong as I thought or even hoped to be…"

ONE OF THE ROLES THAT I TOOK ON AS AN adult was to take care of my mother's lawn. Now my father never maintained our lawn and I was always embarrassed by that. Our yard was never nearly as nice to those of our neighbors. The uneven and overgrown shrubs, splotchy grass, lack of flowers and sometimes tire marks from him driving his cars right through the yard or just parking them there. The general disorder of the surroundings represented the same thing that was going on inside of the house as the outside. I was ashamed. This was symbolic to me because the other dads in our neighborhood took care of their lawns and I assumed took care of their families. We were exposed as being different again.

I know that I consciously keep my own yard so precise as a direct result of how I felt as a child. My children might think I am slightly preoccupied with our yard, but they will never be embarrassed by it. This gave me feelings of inadequacy and inferiority which became heavily rooted in my feelings concerning myself.

For years I would go to my parents' new house to work on the yard. Later my son would come too. We trimmed, weed wacked and cleaned. I was proud of it, and the perennials started to take and grow over the years. The last time

I went there I went alone on a Sunday in June at 7:30 in the morning. This was five years ago. My plan was to get the work done and leave before my father returned from his routine. I went alone and brought several annual flowers and plants, top soil and mulch. I looked forward to doing this nice thing for my mom.

I unloaded my tools, extension cords and equipment and got to work. After an hour, I was on my knees facing away from the house, planting, the day was beautiful and sunny and looking back, it was so symbolic of my whole life. I was proud of what I was doing, and it seemed to be what normal people did. I was excited for my mother to see how nice it was, and she didn't have to be ashamed of her yard like we always were before. But the closer I came to feel a sense of normalcy, the more dysfunctional and hurtful he would become. On this occasion, he did not hold back. I never knew he was even behind me. He walked up a few feet from me. I heard his voice and it was cutting and cold. I felt like I was a small child again. The words were scary and unbelievable. The "*secret*" was never spoken of out loud, not once, never.

"Hey... hey? You know I never hit her!" "She said that I hit her, the liar!" "SHE'S A LIAR!!!, you know that don't you?!!" "You know I never hit her right?!!" "YOU KNOW THAT BITCH IS LYING!!!!"

I have no ability to begin to describe how this impacted me. I have no analogy to explain the feeling. All the air was ripped from my chest. I was weak and if I were standing I doubt that I could have maintained an upright position. I put my hand on the ground. I don't know how much time passed. This was a flashback to myself as a child, I was powerless and could not escape; my heart rate launched, and I could feel myself panting. I looked down at my hand in the dirt holding me up.

I gradually stood and turned around to face him. He is old now in his 70's and he is no longer taller than me, his forearms don't bulge with power and his shoulders are no longer wide, but he was scarier than ever to me. I said nothing, and he kept going with this rant. Louder, echoing against the other houses. I never heard anyone even talk about this, but his denials hurt me. He was erasing my past, invalidating the truth of my life, and he was eliminating what made me the person that I was forced to become.

He then went on to insult my grandparents, his own father and my sister too. Saying nasty and horrible things. He was following me around as I was gathering my things still in shock. He continued ranting. Ugly and dark. Finally, I spoke saying and repeating and gradually yelling, *"I don't have to listen to this! Why are you saying this?"*

"Yes, you do! You HAVE TO LISTEN!!! *Everyone thinks she is the good one. Everyone is on her side. I stayed! I am the good one! How would you feel if some man's wife called you to tell you your wife was sleeping with her husband?!* ***That happened to me! I stayed! That is what she is! You have to listen! She was out having an affair and I stayed! That happened to ME! She's a liar! I STAYED!!! THAT BITCH!!"***

He went on how my grandfathers were not strong or good men, that his father was a thief, how my sister is a disappointment and that there is *"something wrong"* with her.

I calmly looked him straight in the eye as we stood in his front yard with all the flowers that I planted and slowly said, *"Why do you want to hurt me so much?"* There were a few seconds of silence and with that, he finally stopped and walked away.

I think that I always had a tiny hope, a thread of hope that someday I might have a semblance of a "normal family" component. When my father confirmed the affairs of my mother, it resulted in a slow decompensation of refused acceptance that I never had any time of a *"family"* nor will have anything remotely like that. Not with them.

I collected up my tools, packed my truck and I left as fast as I could. I have never been back there and as of this writing five years later, I have never seen nor spoken to him other than in court. He is a grudge holder, and he made me into one too.

Over the years and with a challenging amount of effort and fear, I have learned to apologize. I can share my feelings and respect another's point of view. I can get in my truck, drive to therapy and strive to be a better person, better husband, better father and better man. I am not ashamed or embarrassed anymore, but just the opposite. I am proud. He is a coward. He fears the truth and terrified the knowledge and reality of what his legacy truly is. I am so many more times the man he thinks and declares himself to be. I celebrate my commitment to my improvement and therapy now and never miss a session, although the first few months was a battle for me to go. Now I look forward to the challenges and can see how far I have come.

Chapter 16:

PERCEPTION

"Jimmy, no families are perfect"

OVER THE WEEKS AND MONTHS THAT FOL-
lowed were a progressive confusion over how and why I
was feeling so depressed, disorganized and extremely and
consistently sad. Periods of pain and crying, perseverating
on questions that I had no answers to. I tried speaking with
my mother, but the closer I got to the true origins the more
forgetful and evasive she became. She then began to repeat
the directives of my youth. How *"good,"* I have it, *"how many
people have it worse than me,"* and the last one, *"you need to
throw some water on your face, stop thinking about this, and
just move on."*

There is one thing that I realized can summarize this
entire process about how conditioned and enslaved by her
opinions and approval I was.

When my children were growing up we always took my
mother on vacation with us. Many beach vacations, cruises,
trips to places like Puerto Rico and Bahamas, which all produced several photographs of "Grandma" holding my young
children. My mother has several scars on her right forearm
that my father is responsible for. These scars are clearly visible. They become more prominent in summer. Prior to my
refusal to continue my life the way it was going, I NEVER
<u>saw</u> those scars. Those scars were never observed in my

conscious perception. They never registered or were visible to me. I completely blanked them out.

Now, that is all I see. It was black and white. When I tried to talk with her later, I brought up the scars and asked her about them. Her response? *"Well, it's just one…"*

I have continued to attempt to navigate through his moods and verbal insults throughout my adulthood. I tried to help my mother in ways that I could in order to try and make her life better, easier. I now know that she consciously and unconsciously manipulated me into her world, their world. I don't blame her since I have learned that it is a textbook reaction in the classic co-dependent personality. I would take care of small tasks and let my disorder run wild and try to "normalize" their lives, solve their problems and take them on as my own. I was that delusional in my own abilities. She was going to change him when she married him, and I was going to change them both. So many feelings of anger and sadness, hope and desperation and for what?

Leading to my breaking point with him included my wife's diagnosis with thyroid and lymph node cancer. This was very scary to me. Extremely frightening to think about and possibilities that terrified me. How this would affect her, how it would impact our children, and the horrible thoughts and decisions that come with receiving a diagnosis like that.

She had the surgery, then the radiation and for the weeks that followed my father never once attempted to help. Just the contrary, he made my life truly a proverbial "living hell" during that time. I always felt that he didn't care for me or loved me, but now I knew it. I truly believe that he is incapable of loving anyone. I was having nightmares where I had to tell my daughter that mommy wouldn't be with us anymore, waking up crying and my father was causing a real nightmare in our lives. My wife's surgeon told me, *"stress is her number one enemy."* My father had the talent and ability to become the number one stressor in our lives, and he positioned himself right there.

Chapter 17:

PAUL McCARTNEY

*"I always thought there was one world for me and
one for everybody else..."*

I BEGAN TO EXPERIENCE A PROGRESSING
issue that was unknown to me. Leaving the house became an
anxiety inducing bargaining session with myself that could
last for days and weeks leading up to the scheduled event.
Rarely was the outcome as horrible as I mentally predicted
it to be. Usually the exact opposite, then I would perseverate
for days after wondering why I did this to myself. I would
bargain and debate internally hoping my wife might be sick,
and I could use that as an excuse to not have to go, or maybe
it would be canceled, or something would arise that would
give me a reason to politely decline.

Many times, I would make up an excuse that I had to
drive myself thus have my own car for an escape. I even
would park facing out, so I knew that I would not be blocked
in. These tricks helped me and for a while, it was enough to
get me to attend these outings or dinners. Some occasions
would be interesting to me, but as the date crept closer the
weight and stress that I created would build and the "fun"
idea then became a frightening stress-inducing burden that
would become the focus of my thoughts, and sometimes
dreams too, and confine me in a constant struggle about

what could be. If I knew that certain friends were going to be there that was a tremendous relief and support for me.

This is exactly where I was when I hit my bottom.

Several weeks before the event, my friend, Alex, asked my wife and I to attend the Paul McCartney concert with his wife and a group of his friends. These people were associates of mine, but not "friends" in the sense that I would feel comfortable with them. We agreed to go because it was exciting, and we always had a nice time with Alex and his wife. I had known him since boyhood and he was my football coach's son. The two of them chose my wife and I to be the godparents of their son. Alex is not comfortable with the specifics of my issues, but he is an unconditional voice of support and is often a welcomed comedic relief for me.

As the days past and the planning progressed, plans were made to have dinner at a local restaurant in downtown Pittsburgh in a private room and we then had a private box at the concert as well. My wife and I do not usually have access to things like that, so I am sure that was a motivator too. The time length of the event was increasing, which slowly started to become an issue for me. Then I found out that there were going to be more people there, many who I never met before, and it was going to be a birthday party as well. Well, the intensity of all these things began to grow and my wife even mentioned maybe not attending the dinner part, but I struggled on. My instincts and my gut feeling were telling me that this was too much for me. I don't know right now why I was so committed to this event, but I wish I hadn't been.

The date finally arrived. My wife and I got dressed up and drove downtown to meet everyone at the restaurant. On the way there, Alex texted me. He said that his wife was not going to attend at all and that he was not going to the dinner. He said that we would just meet him at the concert. Alex said he was going to bring his Dad in his wife's place.

I am was anxiety ridden to start off the whole day and now, my friend who is also my connection to all these people is not even attending, nor is his wife, and now my high school football coach is coming too. Coach Wayne has always been extremely supportive of me and has watched me from afar since I was 14 years old. He has gone to great lengths to help me throughout my life, but I embellished his role and inflated him to super-human status. I created a person and a relationship that went far beyond all the encouragement and help he gave me. I intensified his role to be astronomical and humanly impossible in my life. I made him into the man I wanted as a father in my mind. He took the gifts up to the altar in my wedding, helped me get into Notre Dame and helped me get me first coaching job. He wrote several letters of recommendation for me too, but no human could be the person I had created in my head.

As I was driving to dinner, I began to physically feel the pressure of the news I just heard. I could feel my heart beating, I was sweating, and it felt like I was shaking. I think my wife talked about going to another restaurant. I tried to hide what was going on physically and emotionally — I have no idea why I insisted on going to this dinner. Rational thought was gone, my heart raced faster, and faster, and involuntary twitching movements began in my hands and eyelids. I never had anything experience like this before.

I didn't even remember that we had a valet park the car until I later recounted this event. I can't remember walking in the building let alone into the private dining room. I was having a panic attack in a slow evolution. There was one friend, Ethan, who I hoped would be there and he was, but aside from him there were 20 people, most of them I never met before. This restaurant had the private wine cabinets for VIP diners and my friend, Ethan, had one of those. He insisted that I try his wine and I did, but I was still shaking while at the same time I am meeting people and attempting small talk. Trying to remember names and hide my trembling hands. There was nothing at all comfortable to me. Nothing. My body was perspiring, and I could feel the sweat rolling down my back. I thought if I had a drink it would settle me down. I ordered a "vodka on the rocks" like my father-in-law does. Dinner was not for some time since this was a sched-uled "cocktail hour" and several people were buying drinks for each other.

Quickly, as people were buying drinks there were two more vodkas in front of me. I survived dinner and then we left to walk to the arena for the concert. I remember walking there and going into the arena to the private seating area. Of course, there was a bar directly behind our box.

Finally, Alex and his Dad came. All our seats were in two rows, one elevated above the other. I was trying to "fit in," trying to "not be me." I went out to the bar and got another vodka. I wasn't scared anymore now, but no one was drinking as much as me either. I remember laughing and messing around, but the people I was with didn't want to do that especially since one of the greatest artists of all-time was playing some of the classic Beatles songs. A few people were laughing too, but more were not. I am sure I was the loudest and I was asked to calm down, but I guess I didn't do that. What happened next took me a very long time to understand and process. I no way am I defending myself or making an excuse. I am certain that I was the problem.

I must have said the wrong thing to a guy that everyone there knew had a quick temper. Suddenly, in a split second, I was on the ground. He tackled me. I was shocked and extremely embarrassed. My wife was looking down at me. I felt so small, so defeated, so ashamed, so alone, so hurt, so ruined

My Coach looked over and uttered, *"too much alcohol,"* nothing more and disappointingly looked away. No one came to me. I got up alone and my wife said to me, *"Come on, we should go."* I was lost, I was empty. We went home and that was it.

The next morning, I reviewed and repeated the events of the previous evening over and over. I rehashed and tortured myself, replaying it endless times. All alone, crying, angry, condemning and coming up with no answers just blank. No one called me the next day. I waited and waited for someone to call me and minimize the damage. Soothe me somehow, tell me it was okay, someone that could help me. I was so low, so far down, so black and dark.

Finally, Alex called and then Ethan did later, which I will forever be grateful, but that didn't alleviate what was debilitating me. I was beyond drained and so weak, this was my lowest point.

No one else called. I was alone. Crying without any certainty of anything.

I realize now why this was so unbearable to me, why it was agonizing, stopping time making the suffering endless and my condition was dire. When I was thrown onto the floor in front of all those people I remember looking up squarely into the eyes of my Coach. There was nothing back. That was my lowest point. I wanted him to rescue me, to reach down and take over, protect me and make everything go away. I created a role for him in my mind and now I expected him to play it, act it out and make it all come true. None of that happened though. He looked down at me with disappointment in his eyes. I was never more alone than that day.

No person could have actually accomplished what I had hoped and yearned for, not my Coach or any other of the people I placed in that role before him. I have been looking for someone to rescue me my entire life, but because of that night, on the floor of that arena, at the Paul McCartney concert, I realized that the only person who could truly "rescue" me was me.

I decided to go to therapy the next day. My wife came home from work and I looked at her, *"I feel like I am going off the rails, something is wrong with me and I can't handle it. I don't know what it is, but it is out of my control. I'm scared."*

Chapter 18:

THERAPY

"Why do you think you are weak?"

I EXPERIENCED SOMETHING THAT I NEVER
had before. I had "panic attack" in public. I had no skills to
identify it or deal with it. I never experienced anything like
that before.

Looking back, I can see that there were indicators that
today I would recognize immediately, but I had no knowledge or understanding then. Leading up to that day, when
I said to my wife, *"I feel like I am going off the rails,"* that was
the worst feeling I ever had, the lowest, the bottom.

When my friend had called me the next day, I could not
explain it to him, I had no words, no ability to describe how
bad it really was. I was very afraid, and I knew I could not
handle it by myself. My children needed me, and I had to
do something.

My history was so fragmented and frightening, it took
a long process to retrace, reconnect and identify the factual
accounts. There was no preparation, no thought or planning
involved on what I did next. I woke up, opened my iPad and
searched. Minutes later I found a therapy service and called.
The receptionist asked what I was "looking for" and I had a
lifetime of answers to that question. I responded, *"anything
as soon as possible."* She told me they had an open appointment possibility if I "didn't mind having a female therapist"

and that some men requested male therapists. *"No, that's fine. Does she have experience in child abuse?"* That was the first time I admitted that to anyone in my life.

The night before I went to my first appointment, I did not sleep. I wasn't sure I was going to go. I know my wife probably doubted it too. I lied to myself that I could handle it and it will get better. Driving there was hard. I hated it, but I knew that felt that I was *"off the rails"* in every aspect of my life and things were way out of my control. I pounded the steering wheel, white-knuckled and bargained telling myself that I didn't need to do this.

The first appointment was a blur. I cried and had no idea if I made any sense. When it was leaving my therapist asked me if I was going *"to come back,"* if I was *"going to go away,"* did I *"feel like leaving?"* At first, I didn't understand, but then I realized that she was *"contracting for safety"* with me. No, I wasn't going to run away. I had been running all my life, I was tired and raw. There was no way I wasn't coming back. No way. Not now.

The weeks that followed slowly got better. I hated going there. I mean really HATED it. I was angry that I had to go there, that my father created all of this in my life. I bought the books I saw on my therapist's shelves. I learned that I have CPTSD (Complex Post Traumatic Stress Disorder) and that my story is not uncommon. That many men like me walked through very similar paths. Sadly, I found it comforting that there were other's like me. I found many support sites online including *Isurvive.org* that were and are extremely helpful. Twitter has many P.T.S.D/C.P.T.S.D. support sites too that I follow daily.

The progress was – and is–very slow. I kept reading, writing in my journal and wanting to relax–not think about it anymore. I learned interesting things that resonated with me.

All my friends in grade school played baseball and basketball, and I did as well. I liked being on teams, being part of the social group, I think, was more of the attraction for me. I never excelled or was very talented, but I was dependable and hopefully, a good team mate. When I progressed to high school and college the focus became all football. Although my athletic ability was limited I wanted to be a part of a team, the challenge and the work involved.

Football attracts boys with backgrounds like mine. It requires a tremendous amount of time with practice, weight lifting, films and several extending activities, fund raisers, etc. that would keep me away from home. I was very fortunate to have coaches available to me that were excellent role models which I was not so subconsciously seeking. I realized recently looking back and thinking about football in my life as a player in high school and college football, and high school coach for over 20 years. I enjoyed those times and repeatedly hear about the "love of the game." I never "loved" the game. I liked it very much but what was much more important to me was being part of the team, being a part of the program. Football gave me a sense of belonging, a place to go to and spend time with positive male role models. I loved having a place that was mine, a part of a unit that was measured fairly and people really cared for me and about me. I stay in touch with my college coaches too.

I started trying to explain my life to Coach Wayne recently and he stopped me and asked me a question. He said, *"In all your years of coaching did you ever have a player who was a good kid, hard worker and solid program guy?"* *"Sure"* I responded. *"Now, did you ever have a kid like that and you never met his dad?"* I had to think about that for a while. *"Yeah, I have".* He quickly looked at me and said, *"Jimmy, that was you."*

Later, I too became a high school football coach and worked with many young men with similar backgrounds. Although I would not share any specifics of my life, I think they could see it in me. Many of my former players stay in contact and have shared their stories with me. I attend their weddings and see them begin their own families. There is a positive in everything and maybe my childhood experiences provided me with insights to help and support them. One of my former players asked me to be in his wedding party–15 "twenty somethings" and a 50-year-old! That was extremely emotional to me and I am very fortunate to be thought of that way. On the wedding day one of the groomsmen who played with the groom in college said to me, *"the last guy I want at my wedding is my high school coach."*

I started to locate and contact people from my past who knew me when I was young. Neighbors and friends, people that I have not spoken to in decades. All these things helped me. I was worried at first what they may say about me, but I realized that was my father speaking. I found so many people who were so positive and complimentary to me. One ex-friend of my fathers said to me, *"Jimmy, I have been waiting years to talk with you."*

One day in therapy I learned something that really helped me. Upon the completion of a session, my therapist asked me how I *"felt."* I responded *"weak"* like I had so many previous times when she asked me that question. I felt weak because I had to go there, had to still deal with all of this, and she sharply cut me off. My therapist is extremely professional and always maintains a therapeutic, professional demeanor. This was different. She looked at me and said, *"Do you know how many men your age who come here and sit in that chair who aren't court ordered or have a DUI or a divorce pending?"* *"No"*, I answered in a soft monotone. She looked directly in the eye and just said, *"None, just you. You are the only one."*

Then I started to understand how strong that I truly am. I realized how hard it is to pursue this kind of help and go against social stigmas, what I was taught, instincts, etc., to address what I need. I told my therapist that I felt that I had what I called *"anger reservoirs"* inside of me and I did not know where they came from or why. That was a true *"breakthrough"* for me.

As time passed and I progressed deeper into therapy I began to look forward to my appointments and feel very positive about my efforts there.

This would not become a secret in my life, just the opposite.

Chapter 19:

FIRST APPOINTMENT

"I was way beyond scared...."

ONE OF MY POSITIONS IN MY FORMER CAREER
as an R.N. was as the Assistant Nurse Clinical Manager of
a Dual Diagnosis Unit at Western Psychiatric Institute at
the University of Pittsburgh. Our in-patient unit focused on
those with a serious psychiatric diagnosis and a chemical
dependency. I have been exposed to and personally worked
with hundreds of addicts. I know the "12 Steps." I know
about *"coming clean and making amends."* I never felt I had
any "amends" to make, but I quickly realized that for years
I had a collection of funny stories that I had embellished and
accented about my father that I told welcoming audiences at
work, at parties and in the neighborhood.

I was often asked, *"What's new with your dad?"* and *"How
is he doing?"* It became extremely important to me that I
"come clean" with these people who were important to me,
and I could eliminate my "cover up" and promotion of him.
The list was short, but I scheduled meetings, drove to many
locations and over a few days and weeks I explained how
he wasn't the *"Good Time"* funny guy of those stories that I
told so many times over and over. I told the truth, I shared
the secret. Although I was anxious, I was also relieved and
prepared for the fall- out if necessary.

Most of my friends were extremely supportive. I know how rare it is to have a support network that I have who sincerely care about me. I made a lunch date with a great friend, outstanding educator and ally to explain my story. As I began, my friend Melanie abruptly stopped me and said, "*I know this already. I knew this a year ago.*"

I was shocked, I thought no one knew.

She told me that she met my high school teacher, Mr. Costello, at my house the previous year when we had a small party at our house and they spoke together. She said that "*my teacher*" told her how I used to go to his house and sleep on their sofa. I forgot about that. Mr. Costello never locked his house, so I would go there at different times of the day or night and watch TV, sleep on their couch or just be not in my house.

Melanie said she knew that I was victimized, "*if you had to sleep at your teacher's house I knew that bad things were happening to you.*" She went on to tell me she has been avoiding my father whenever she was in his presence, explaining that she "*never liked him.*"

Isurvive.org. I typed in "*child abuse survivor*" into Google and began to read. I found a few helpful sites, but most were for sexual abuse cases. Gradually, I located *isurvive.org* and read story after story of terrible abuse histories just like mine and worse. I spent hours reading and following the conversations of other people in chat rooms. I decided that I "*didn't have it that bad*" that my story "*was nowhere near as extreme*" as the victims that I was being exposed to on the site. (I later learned that is a normal defense mechanism that abuse victims develop especially since that was the standard line my mother gave me anytime I was upset.)

Then I read that it didn't matter how many times or degree of injury that was caused, abuse was abuse. I attempted to make my initial post on a *"Welcome"* page.

My first sentence went, "*I am not exactly sure if I belong on here…*."

Chapter 20:

DREAMS

"I just want them to stop, I need them to stop...."

MY THERAPY WAS VERY FOCUSED ON attempting to identify and quantify very specific events that I had spent my entire life doing just the opposite. I worked on time lines and tried to quantify events and memories. Unconsciously, I attempted to blend and fuse countless painful memories into one major occurrence. This is a common defense mechanism to combine the most severe and damaging recollections with the objective to minimize anguish.

During this process over weeks and months, I began to have many dreams and severe nightmares. Extremely vivid and detailed that I remembered after I awoken, which was and is very rare for me. In my past, I might remember a handful of dreams each year, and even then, they were just small pieces and short items of no significance aside from the previously mentioned *"Alligator Dream."* The dreams that emerged after I started therapy resulted in from my search to remember where terrifying, chilling and left me powerless.

There was a period of days that I was so afraid to go to sleep that I would stay awake until I was exhausted. Sometimes I would just stay awake, go to *Denny's* at 4:00 a.m. and read. Later that fall, I would return home after the school day and immediately go to sleep. I rarely had nightmares then, during *"naps"* which soon began to replace sleeping at night altogether inconsistently.

During this period, the nightmares were so disturbing they made the mornings totally exhausting and painful. The immediate thoughts upon awakening were physically debilitating, haunting, and then the process of trying to understand them or interpret them became an all-day obsession. My dreams were so sharp and puzzling, extremely thorough and directly focused on the actual abuses and severe violence that was my life so long ago.

Fortunately, in my profession as a teacher, this happened during the summer vacation period, but that also left me with the entire day to wallow in the unknown and torment without anything to occupy and take my mind off it. If this occurred during my school year there would have been no way I could have conducted my classes.

The dreams spurred many memories or scenes which then caused me to chronically try to analyze them and dissect them to identify what, if any of it, was real and question if any of it happened or if they were just nightmares based on these true events. There were many times I had to ask my sister about certain aspects to confirm if they were true, some were, and some were not, however, both outcomes could be equally frightening to me.

I remember some of them and time has helped me grasp them to a point, but to say I understand them is too far of a reach. There was one dream I had during this time which was very troubling. I am lying down on my back in a dark, wet, gray cobblestone street and someone is shooting me several times over and over, and I try to avoid it. I wait for it to stop. Numerous rounds are being fired. Loud. Violent. All around me, at me, in me, but I never die. There was no end, no screaming but an extremely sudden and startling awakening.

I used to look at that negatively, but now I feel it must mean that I can survive, that I did survive. Similarly, one dream was not a nightmare at all but chilling to me none the less. I am a very small boy, 4 or 5 years old. I am walking alone in the daytime in a very stereotypical, foreign country. Something like Bavaria with chalets, people with a specific style of dress and culture very different from me. I cannot speak their language, I cannot communicate with anyone and no one is familiar to me. Nothing happens to me, I am not harmed in anyway, but I am alone, and I cannot find anyone that I know.

In another dream, I find myself a little older in the dark on a stage, I have no idea where I am, and nothing is familiar to me. I have never been in the auditorium nor know anything about the environment or people. I begin to realize that I have been placed in a cast of a play that is in process, I am on the stage and everyone is looking at me. Bright stage lights, a large audience, actors and a director are all looking at me and I have no idea what the play is or what my lines might be. Everyone stops and looking at me waiting…

There are several repetitive dreams that emerge with extreme irregularity. I am in a car with the windows up and the doors are locked, and my father is trying to get me. Walking around the car yelling and threatening me. One that I have is where I am at my father's house, and it is an unlivable sty with no plumbing and filth everywhere. Nothing is clean, no electricity or laundry and there is a small child or several little children there that he is *"watching for a friend."* Sometimes I try to get the children away, and sometimes I have nowhere to go, no place to live and am forced to have to stay there with them.

I have also dreamt that my Grandmother is still alive and living in her home. But when I attempt to see her, I am physically prevented from seeing her. Another is that I am in a fight in a parking lot, yard or field with one or more people. I am violently and aggressively punching and swinging, making contact, but I can never inflict any damage. I cannot make it stop nor subdue my attackers in anyway. This is my most common repetitive dream.

My therapist told me this was "normal" and that it would be temporary. That was the only positive I had at that time. I could not imagine being subjected to this experience without therapy.

Thankfully, I have not had any extreme dreams like that since then. That was a horrible time in my life. My wife said I would yell, walk in my sleep and once, I tried to throw her out of bed. She said she awoke one night to find me standing in front of our bedroom window talking. I am very thankful that it stopped. It is horrible just thinking about that time in my life. I still have odd and uncomfortable dreams, but nothing like that period in my life.

Periodically my wife will say I was "*whimpering*" or having jerking motions in my sleep. I would wake up and my jaws would ache from being clenched tightly. Sometimes I wake up on the floor. Going to sleep and waking up are still not the most pleasant times of my day, but it is improving, although very slowly. I find it upsetting that I can't remember all the details of my dreams to the degree I want to, so I can figure out the meanings more clearly.

Chapter 21:

FLASHBACKS

"I need to give up hope that my past and my life could have been different..."

YELLOWSTONE WAS THE DESTINATION FOR our family vacation and at that point, I had no personal knowledge of why I reacted and behaved the way I did. I knew that I was different, but little insight beyond that.

We were driving to the sights of the National Park each day and having a great time together. Near the end of the trip we went to see the Old Faithful geyser. I then took my daughter to the "Old Faithful Gift Shop" and I said to her, *"You can have anything you want."* Immediately after the last word came out of my mouth, I had to physically hold onto the counter. I went numb for a split second, got cold and light-headed, then looked around to see if anyone was looking at me. It took some time to gather myself together and regain my surroundings. It scared me. I had a split-second vision of being in gift shops as a child. Not a specific memory, but a frightening and extremely disturbing feeling.

The word *"flashback"* was not understood by me at that time, nor did I even think of something like it, but that is exactly what it was. When they would occur my mood changed, quickly and negatively. I become irritated and then would perseverate about it for hours afterwards usually making those around me uncomfortable.

These experiences continue, but I understand and am more aware of it now. There is no indicator or preceptory event to these occurrences and they present in no particular time frame nor mood. If I see handwriting that looks like my mother's, the smell of motor oil or engine grease, old Pepsi bottles or the sound of a sneeze or slamming door, it can freeze me into a period of stillness and uncertainty. All sensory stimulations stop. No sound, no awareness exactly like a vacuum effect just for a few seconds — but it feels much longer.

Sometimes when I do manual work, I look at my hands and for an instant, they are his hands, like they are not attached to me, like they are <u>his</u> hands. Sometimes my voice inflection or a physical movement reminds me of him. I am a "junior" and thus cursed with his name. Periodically, his mail comes to my address, the bank will need to clarify an account and many other reminders.

I wished I would have changed it. I used to think about that, using my Grandmother's maiden name which is my daughter's middle name. These are things I must deal with it, hopefully, in time they will all fade away.

Chapter 22:

MOURNING

*"I experience a small 'funeral' almost every day
of my life…"*

MY PERSONAL EXPERIENCES WITH DEATH
were very limited. I had just arrived in South Bend, IN to
begin my graduate program at Notre Dame when I found
out my Grandmother died of a massive stroke. I was very
sad, but at the same time I was comforted by the fact that
she did not have to suffer in any way. She had told me many
times of her fear of a prolonged uncontrollable illness. I was
happy that she never had to go through that kind of turmoil.
She was so full of life and that is exactly how I remember her.

My last surviving grandparent died right after my
son was born. My Grandfather was a WW II veteran and
a very humble, caring man. I knew him very well and we
shared many great memories together. He and I traveled to
Bradenton, FL to watch the Pirates in spring-training in 1986
and to Canton, OH to see the NFL Hall of Fame on the 50th
Anniversary of D-Day. There were many, many other trips,
games and visits. The days leading up to his death of respi-
ratory and cardiac ailments thanks to a 60-year *Lucky Strike*
habit were very difficult for him. The day he told me that he
didn't care about watching the Steeler game, I knew that his
desire to live was waning. He was too weak to walk into the
next room where his giant wooden floor model television

was placed five- feet in front of his recliner. He was so frail then, I even offered to carry him. He politely declined and a few days later he was in a hospice.

The pain was constant, and I could not position him in any way that it didn't hurt, even with 10 pillows. He was a proud man, didn't complain but I could tell nothing was working. My mother and uncle, his only children, were so sad and worn. They were like small children as they waited for their last parent to pass and for them to grudgingly stutter into the next stage of their lives. My experiences working as an orderly and then as a registered nurse with liver transplants included many cases that involved every stage of death. I knew there was no improvement from the situation my Grandfather was in at that point.

I spoke with my mother and explained what could be done. It was late in the evening. I remember the charge nurse was a large man, dark with a long, black ponytail. He was excellent at his craft, professional and I think he knew exactly what I was about to say. He made the connection and received the verbal order from the M.D. on call. I watched him hook up the morphine drip to my Grandfather's IV and I knew that he would never be in pain again. I loved him and wish I told him that.

I have attended the funerals of students of mine who were in accidents, over-doses and extremely premature terminal illnesses, but prior to my current situation, the saddest and most hurtful experience with death was the miscarriage of our second child. I was so sad, so powerless and truly mournful. The situation was, which I found out later, probably very like many couples. My wife felt something *"wrong"*, so we went to the hospital, she miscarried. We went out to dinner on the way home. I couldn't believe how calm my wife was. We took our son with us. While I was presented with this initially I was planning a funeral in my mind. I didn't know if I had to call my church or my cousin who is a funeral home director.

We had just lost a child, our baby. We weren't having a baby anymore. Our baby died. I said nothing. If my wife could handle it, I wasn't going to cause any issues for us. I called my parish priest. I really had no idea what to do but I assumed that is what a "Catholic" does. I was grieving then and unconsciously at the time I experienced the stages of denial, anger, acceptance, etc.

When I was 11 and in the sixth grade, I was an altar boy. Once, I was sitting in class and the pastor of our church and school, Father Walters came to the door of my class and asked for me by name. He took me across the parking lot without a single word spoken. He never spoke to any of us anyhow, so that wasn't unusual. It was a weekday, so it wasn't a wedding and it wasn't 7:00 a.m. so it wasn't our daily morning mass either. I was going to serve a funeral. I know this will sound horrible, but I was just a little kid. This was a "good thing," I got to get out of school and most likely someone was going to tip me so that meant baseball card money to me. We walked in and then I went to the deep rear of the sacristy to get dressed. First, my long black robe and then the white cassock over top, same as every time before. Then the feeling changed, no hearse was outside and there were no people. No crying old ladies, no pallbearers and no flowers. This was not how typical funerals appeared from my perspective. I didn't say anything and didn't dream of asking the old priest about it. He never talked. I don't know how long we waited there, a little boy and a notoriously grumpy aged pastor standing side-by-side staring at the front glass door of the church.

Finally, a station wagon pulled up and a well-dressed man walked up to us with a small white cooler-like container and gave it to the priest. The man drove away and the two of us walked down to the altar. The church was empty aside from the two of us. Father placed the white box on a small stand just in front of the altar. I carried the Holy Water and aspergilla which I held when the Priest blessed the coffin, but there was no coffin. He began the ceremony and I followed.

It was more concentration with just one server, and I didn't want to get a judging, dirty look if I messed up.

I don't know how long it took me to figure out what was occurring. I knew it wasn't training because I passed all my altar boy "tests," and Father Greg handled all of that. The small "cooler" was a baby and we were performing a funeral mass for a baby. When we were done the man in the black Lincoln station wagon came back and was standing in the rear of the church waiting for us. He took the small container away, I changed alone and then walked back to class. No one spoke to me, the priest didn't explain anything to me, there was no tip, and I was left with more issues with the church than I woke up with that day.

Now, I assumed that I would have to do something like that since our baby died too. My wife was not that far along so the procedure at the hospital left me with no physical "baby" even if I wanted a funeral. I often wonder what is exactly performed and you would think that since I was a nurse, that I would know.

I didn't know, and I really didn't want to know either, but I still think about it. I called my parish priest anyhow and made an appointment. We were new to the parish and I had no relationship with the man but somehow, he, the priest, was going to help me. We met for a few minutes. Waste of my time. I was grieving alone.

The point of this whole section is mourning and death. I had many experiences with death as a child, suicide, performing funerals as an altar boy, I worked at a funeral home as a teenager, and later as an orderly and registered nurse in a major teaching hospital. This process has taken me to the most precise and sorrowful reality of mourning the loss of a loved one.

I now realize and can feel for people who I see so impacted and heart felt in their grieving. I understand that now. I know what that feels like, how the reminders take you to that time, the regrets and the wishes to have them back. These feelings are no longer foreign to me. I know how true loss feels.

I mourn for me.

I mourn for the little boy that I was supposed to be. If any pictures do exist of me, and there are few because I never wanted my photograph taken, I never smiled.

I mourn for what was taken away from me and how I might have been if I didn't have to witness, to have to hide, to experience and to cry.

I mourn for me as a child when I thought about catching butterflies. When my father would block the front door with his body holding us inside, terrifying us. When I was 5 and went to kindergarten. When I was 6 when my mom took me to Peanut League Baseball while the other boys had their fathers there with them. When I made my First Communion and my mother dressed me. It was over after that. I was no longer going to be the person I was meant to be. My life was taken away by the ugliness of screaming and threats, fear, embarrassment and lies, violence and banishment, false hopes and fake smiles and wondering why? *Why me?*

That is my most personal experience with death and mourning.

Chapter 23:

BLAME

*"I know that this was done **TO** me and I did not deserve any of it".*

THE STAGES OF THIS MANIPULATION AND control never appeared to me consciously at any time in my life. As a child, I assumed my parents "stayed together" because of my sister and me. This guilt combined with being raised Catholic and attending Catholic schools, I became a master of keeping secrets and creating even more guilt for myself.

My parents have been currently "married" for over 50 years. They did not get married because my mother was pregnant, which I assumed immediately when I learned of that possibility. They were married in January 1964. I know it is in January, but I honestly don't know the actual date. We never celebrated it, no special dinners, no parties, and no cards. None from my sister or me, none from my grandparents, and none from each of them. Not once.

I was born in June of 1966. From my inquiries and stories that I have heard or overheard, my parents set their wedding date according to my father's interpretation of the Vietnam draft policies of that time. Since married men supposedly had their draft number "dropped" on the draft list they moved their wedding date up and to save from any public scorn they did not have me until considerable time after that.

My father never formally applied for a draft deferment, but he thought it was automatic.

We lived within six houses on the same block as all my grandparents, aunts, uncles, etc. I was the first-born grand-child on both sides of my family. My father's family was Irish, and my mother's was German so both sides of my family felt they were both *"marrying down"* which resulted in varied layers of dissatisfaction from both of the sides of my family on our little street.

Responsibility is a trait that is lacking in many forms in my father's family, several grudges and scandals, emotional traumas and incidents lace their history. Everyone had their secrets, but none like mine. However, actual responsibility for who was at fault is virtually nonexistent. There are many tales which by the telling and re-telling have become "fact" that does not continue the actual truth but is exonerates them from having to address anything. He would project almost anything possible onto me. Once out of nowhere he screamed at me, *"You took her on all those fancy vacations and now she won't go anywhere with me,"* blaming me for their totally failed relationship.

Then you just tuck it away, never talk about it, blame someone else and then erase it like it never happened until one of the needs to draw it like a lethal emotional weapon to attack.

My father was the angriest person I ever saw, he had the most piercing yell and he was never, ever responsible for anything. Everyone else was wrong, they had an agenda against him and he made all the rules.

He always kept us all on an intense surveillance of all our social contacts. Anyone that could be a threat to him or expose him for the abusive perpetrator that he truly was, would be attacked by him and thus distanced from us. He isolated us from them and from each other too if neces-sary. Resistance of this or any kind of escape from it was impossible.

I am slowly learning and accepting that this was not my fault, it was never my fault and it all existed long before I was ever born. This is the exact opposite from what I had concluded from my earliest memories onward as I was left alone to try to configure some explanation for it. I always assumed that all these problems were occurring because of me.

Today, I have no baseline of any sense of calm or comfort. That is a lengthy process that takes my conscious effort and skill. I get angry at myself for being angry or that I will never be NOT be angry. I asked my therapist once, *"When will I be done?"* but I have learned there is no quick fix, this is a slow progression. This is a learning evolution that cannot be speeded up. That was very hard for me to accept.

The first year I restricted him from my life and home, he called me regarding Christmas Eve asking me if he could come to our house with my family. The first few seconds and sentences were about him, bargaining, manipulating and demanding that **HIS** needs be met. He said that he is *"sick"*, *"wants his family back"*, *"doesn't want to be alone."*

I told him that I was going to ask him one question. I asked him very directly the same question I asked him years ago in his front yard, *"Did you ever hit my mother?"* and then he went on the attack screaming at me. He took no responsibility, expressed zero regret, denies his actions and his statements.

I screamed back that it was time to *"**Man up, take responsibility!**"* *"You are a coward! Everything you say that you stand for is a lie."* *"You're a fraud and a hypocrite."* *"You're the one that isn't a man!"* I yelled, *"Do not ever contact me or my family, come to my house and delete our numbers!"* and hung up.

My mother's response to this? She would make excuses for him. *"He misses the kids so much"* He is sick." *"He doesn't have anyone."* *"You can't just leave him alone."* *"He is all alone."* She would repeat the justifications that she had told me so many times as a child, *"We had a nice house though,"* and *"No families are perfect."* I realized this is the same manipulation scheme that she used to keep me in her control my whole life. She positions herself to be the victim and I as her eternal support system that includes the guilt trips that I am the only one that has concerns over the situation.

Anytime there was an event or party that we had to attend was going to result in a problem. My father hated anything like that. The problem would start days before and just progress to the eruption. My mother would have to set all his clothes out and pamper and coddle him throughout the whole process. We would have to prepare who would "watch" him because he couldn't be left alone out of fear of what he might say or do. He has offended the food, people's races or religions with off-color and offensive statements. He is a politically incorrect potential for a problem at any time or setting. For example, if we were attending anything where my mother's coworkers might be it was well known that my father was not allowed to talk to any of them.

This became an issue at my wedding that was repeated over and over as a joke and funny story that I even told myself many times. Today, I can see just how frightening and delusional we all were. The day before my wedding we were in the lobby of a beautiful hotel in Chicago as I watched taxis and airport limos bringing my friends from all over the country to join us. This was one of the greatest times of my life, seeing my friends from all the periods of my life together in one place. Literally out of the corner of my eye, I saw my father on a sofa sitting with my future father-in-law. They met twice before and never alone. He was alone! No one was *"watching"* him!

Here is how my father-in-law explains their interaction. My father stated to him, *"You don't have anything to worry about, you know"?* My father-in-law did not understand what my father was talking about. My father went on, *"Well, you don't have to worry because I raised my boy right. He won't hit her or anything like that."*

Now years later, I can understand how disturbing and deeply demented the entire interaction was. My father never had any individual contact with this man prior to this and that is the statement he came up with? To insinuate that he *"raised"* me is an insult beyond any comprehension and to bring up the image of physically beating this man's daughter the day before her wedding…

That is where I was then. My family hiding what we are in public, in plain view using lies, humor, misdirection and a constant façade so no one would find out.

His actions were his lessons for me, he beat my mother repeatedly which she has admitted to under oath in court. My father, and I quote, when I confronted him in court about repeatedly beating my mother in front of me stated, *"I do not recall ever doing that."*

Chapter 24:

CAPTIVITY

*"I know I need to stop wishing and hoping that my
past could have been different..."*

THIS WORD *"CAPTIVITY"* BRINGS SEVERAL
extreme visions and scenes in my mind. I imagine it would
be the same for many people. I think of those women that
were held for years in Cleveland, chained and imprisoned in
the basement of that lunatic, or of prisoners of war, like John
McCain, Vietnam, Bataan and torture.

When I was very young, I can remember being alone,
especially in the mornings. These thoughts have become
much clearer as I was raising my children. While watching
them I identified aspects that were, thankfully, very different
from mine. Little reminders or a comparison would appear
occasionally. Slowly the details and specifics of the severe
differences from my present home and family to the events
of my past began to emerge. Those memories were not "little"
nor pleasant.

I knew if my parents' bedroom door was closed that was
a bad sign. The yelling and screaming behind it scared me.
Usually it was open, wide open, always. The house did not
have "wall-to-wall" carpeting in the bedrooms, so the carpet
was not cut cleanly and it overlapped the thresholds pre-
venting the bedroom doors from closing completely. The
cheap hollow wooden door to my bedroom could not close

at all. The house was a small six room, two stories. The stairs were in the middle and all three-bedroom doors faced each other, my sister's room was next to mine and my parents' bedroom was 8-feet across the hall.

Some Saturday morning's their door would be completely closed. I would silently creep downstairs, we only had one television but at my earliest memory I knew to be silent. Sometimes one of them would leave the house completely and the other would stay in bed for long periods of time. Later I learned that my mother took anti-depressants and other medications throughout my life. She referred to this as "*doctoring.*"

In earlier stages of therapy, I would have memories just pop into my head. Memories that I previously could not recall would emerge and become clearer. Recently, I was driving my daughter to her practice and while sitting at a red light, a horrifying memory pierced through me like an arrow, it physically impacted me. I clenched the steering wheel, stunned. "*Daddy, it's green,*" my daughter gently reminded me. I have sat through green lights before; my mind is challenged somehow and suddenly the horn of the driver behind me brings me back. I know I have done it alone with no one around because the conditioned response of when the light turns yellow and I am at a standstill confirms it for me.

One specific memory was one of those Saturday mornings when I was a child. The door of my parent's bedroom was closed. My sister wasn't born yet. The morning progressed, and I was downstairs watching cartoons in my underwear because I never had pajamas. My father routinely would wear just underwear around the house, so I really did not know differently.

I was 5 years old. I remember looking up the stairs repeatedly to see if their door was open yet. The cartoons were over. I was hungry and was not able to provide for myself. I must have gone into the kitchen trying to find something that I could reach at that time. The sight of hotdogs in the refrigerator must have been appealing to me. I took one out.

Uncooked and cold. I ate half of it before it was no longer palatable to me. I began to become scared, what would I do with it? I couldn't throw it away in the kitchen because if he would see that it might set him off. He would routinely go through the garbage and trash to see what my mother threw out. He would drag it back in the house throwing things and screaming at her about one item or another. How no one appreciated anything, how hard he worked to pay for everything. *"Who threw this out???! I worked for this! Who do you think paid for this!"*

I knew that I couldn't dispose of it there. Somehow, I came up with an idea that I would go outside and hide it somewhere. This was very radical. I grew up in the city and I was not allowed outside by myself.

I crept down the basement stairs and out the back door, still only wearing my underwear. I went around the back of the house around the side, it was very sunny out and I assume it was around 11:00 a.m. The big garbage cans outside were steel fifty-gallon drums painted red primer on a concrete slab. I couldn't reach them nor lift the lid, I would not have even tried that. I was frightened and ashamed. I knew I should not be outside in my underwear. I was scared holding a half-eaten, uncooked, raw hot dog on a very nice sunny day. I tried to hide behind this big steel drum and figure out what to do. My neighbor saw me! I threw the hot dog behind the cans and ran inside! I ran up to my room! I was terrified, convinced that the neighbor would tell my father and then who knows what might happen.

I don't remember anything else after that except I now had another secret to keep.

After a few weeks of reviewing and contemplating that memory, the concept of captivity came back to me. I have read multiple case studies or personal accounts of people like me that refer to an aspect of "captivity" in their lives. The issue of *"captivity"* seemed way too common in those accounts but now, I suddenly understood.

I can see that he controlled everything in our lives. The money, the TV, the thermostat, the mood, our whereabouts inside and outside of the house, what we ordered and even what we said. He routinely would look at me and state, *"I OWN YOU."* He could go further than that, *"When I die I will come back and haunt you. You remember that!"*

I was 10 years old. That was repeated to me until the last day before I cut all ties with him, basically my whole life.

I couldn't imagine how anyone could love me, that is how he made me feel.

Many, many…. too many times after he would go off screaming, swinging, threatening and terrifying me and the aftermath would result in him just lying down in his work clothes, greasy and dirty with his big work boots on.

He would do this immediately wherever he was.

The kitchen floor, the dining room, hallway, in front of the television or in front of the door. I could not estimate how many times this occurred. I spent years trying to make it "once" in my head as a defense mechanism. These times were just hell. We would have to sit, hide in silence until he would gradually, at best get up and leave, or if something set him off he would just start it up all over again.

One of these times specifically came to me. He was screaming coming up the steps. I hid, and he went after my mother the opposite of my room. Then he laid down across the top of the staircase blocking the stairs and the bathroom. Face down, greasy and dirty clothes and boots all over the carpet. I could smell him, the motor oil and grease removing ("*Gojo*") hand cleaner. I was waiting until it was over. I was under my bed along the wall. The screaming was complete and now the shutdown antics were on. I hoped he would be sleeping, but this was just another way to threaten and control us. If anyone walked by him or tried to step over him he could go off, start up all over again and usually worse.

Now looking back, exactly how long did this go for? I wouldn't know how to estimate it. Fifteen minutes? An hour? The length of time didn't matter to a crying, terrified little boy under his bed. Maybe just barely 6 years old. It seemed like years to me, endless. I was so scared. Opening my door would be insane, I would never have dreamed of it. Not unless I heard the boots going down the stairs. I couldn't go out there. He was literally inches away. The feeling of being smacked or kicked was well known to me by that time. I was so afraid of him. Waiting and waiting and waiting in total silence.

My memories are vibrant from where my bed was in the room, the lime green and white cheap shag carpeting and how it smelled with my face buried in it. I could see the sun rays on the floor, it was summer.

All the windows were always open. There was no air conditioning. All the neighbors had to hear him. The screaming. The slamming doors. Seeing him aggressively speeding away. The house was on a dead end. The neighbors had to know. My aunts, uncles, grandparents all lived within a mile or two. They had to know what he was doing to us, how angry he is and gets, how violent he becomes. They had to witness the chaos, his temper. I know they had "meetings" about our "problems." I assume my mother was stranded in her room or gone. But I knew, I always knew. No one was coming for me.

And I had to go to the bathroom.

I had to go *"number one."*

There was no way I could risk going out there. I was captive in my own room. Now I understood. Somehow with all these threats, fears and unknowns, I had to do something. Very simply and sadly, I crawled out from under my bed into the far corner of my room, furthest from him. I urinated there right on the floor. It was repulsive and disgusting, and it wouldn't be the only time I was forced to do something like that.

Now I understood what they meant by "captivity".

This was extremely hard for me to realize, accept and remember. Right now, it makes me so sad to have to remember that. I never thought about that ever once before that day when it hit me.

These memories continued though, it did not stop there. My therapist asked me if I ever knocked on their bedroom door when it was closed. The thought of that was not even imaginable. **No *way!*** I never hardly even went into that room ever. There was absolutely no way I would ever knock on that door. If it was closed I knew where they were at least.

I had a little silence, a tiny respite as long as that door stayed closed.

Chapter 25:

NIGHT COURT

"Sir remove your hat when you address the court!"

THERE WERE MULTIPLE OCCASIONS AS AN adult that I had to go to my parent's house when I didn't want to. They were arguing, or my mother needed to see me, etc. Once, to irritate my mother he turned the furnace off. It was in January and it was below 50 in their house when I got there. I could see my breath walking down the hall.

This time I was called to go there was one of the last.

The reason this time? My father took her car keys and cell phone and would not allow her to leave the house. Now, I was going to "rescue" my mother and take her away, have her leave him finally and move in with my family. She would stay with us and we would help her find an apartment, a new car and a new life.

Through my windshield I was watching a long, downhill, little-used street that intersected a major roadway at the end of it. There was a restaurant/bar located at the bottom of that hill and in the parking lot, I was sitting with my mother's brother. We sat there together in the dark waiting. My Uncle and I drove to my mother's house to help her leave him once again. She would move in with me and we would help her finally exorcise herself, and us, of him. Ironically, my father's *"best friend in the world"* lured him out of the house. My Uncle and I sat down the street in a restaurant parking lot with the engine off and watched my father and his friend drive right by us. I did not want my Uncle nor me to go alone to my father's house. I know he has access to guns, friends with guns and worse of all, friends with criminal records and guns.

My Uncle and I removed my mother's things, clothes, flat screen TV that I bought for her, all of her other belongings and we left.

It was that simple.

We just drove away. But, I had been through that before, heard the promises and possibilities only to watch her and all of it just go back to the same. This time it was going to be on my terms.

I told my mother that this was a one-time offer. That I would only do this one time. I would help her get an apartment, a new car, I bought her a timeless plane ticket to Colorado to go to my sister's house any time she wanted to. We talked and made plans. I had one more condition. She would file a police report of his threats.

That night, a school night for me, my mother and I drove to the Robinson Township Police Department. My mother filed a criminal complaint against my father for holding her against her will, threatening to kill her and himself. I never thought she would actually go through with it. That was *"the secret"* that no admitted to, no one discussed, especially her, that all the effort and lies were made over and over for decades to cover up. The police officer asked my mother directly if he was *"physically threatening,"* and *"if he was violent in the past,"* and she answered him truthfully. *"Yes."*

Later, I was in another room and a different police officer asked me if I had a firearm in my house for protection against him. He recommended that I should have one and *"know how to use it."* Upon completion of that interview, the officer directed us and advised up to go immediately to Allegheny County Family Night Court in downtown Pittsburgh to file an emergency Protection from Abuse Order. This would legally protect her and me since she would be staying with me *"permanently."*

I did not expect this. I guess from all my past experiences with them I started to minimize or normalize these incidents as a *"paper cut,"* rather than the ***"gaping wound"*** that it truly was. I made the officer repeat this to my mother to guarantee that <u>she really heard him</u>. We left there around 11:00 p.m. and drove to the city. We walked in through metal detectors and into a stench that smelled like an open toilet. We walked through many other steel doors that all closed behind us. The smell of urine was putrid. Everything was concrete block, gray, dark and cold. We sat and waited.

A woman behind bullet proof glass directed us to sit and we waited and waited. I didn't think my mother would go through with it. I was shocked that we even made it this far. I kept expecting her to leave or my father to walk in, something, anything that would change the path we were on.

After about an hour the bailiff opened a solid steel door that looked like it went to basement or industrial closet and instructed us to come in. There were two rows of steel chairs bolted to the floor and a high wooden desk that rose above us where the judge would sit. The judge's bench and the American flag were high, six or eight feet high, in front of us but they sat behind the floor to ceiling iron bars and reinforced glass that separated us from them.

Finally, the Judge appeared, and she was female. I still had my baseball hat on and she sternly directed me to get it off. *"Sir remove your hat if you are going to address this court!"* She immediately asked why we were there and quickly the judge stopped my response, wanting my mother to answer the questions.

The Judge read the compliant, looked down at us and simply asked my mother, *"Did your husband ever hit you?"*

It seemed like hours went by. I turned and watched my mother, crying, looking at the Judge and then back at my mother. She responded clearly and louder than I expected.... *"Yes."*

I never heard the reality of my life so directly addressed before. I found it so sad and yet so satisfying. I knew it was always wrong, I knew it was all lies and now there was someone in my life finally demanding the truth. In court. Under oath.

Quickly the Judge looked at the bailiff and said, *"I want him out of that house immediately! Tonight!"* My mother began to plead for him. She explained that she was safe with me and that removing my father was unnecessary. There was a short discussion while the Judge listened and said if we come back there she would *"remove him"* and that she would *"not tolerate any discussion then."* We were instructed to have no contact with him and to proceed in 72 hours to follow up on the P.F.A. (Protection from Abuse). We went home to my house and surprisingly, my mother was calmer than I expected.

When we got home, it was well after midnight. A police officer called me. They had gone to my father's house to serve the 72-hour P.F.A. order and inform him of the formal complaint. They removed him from the house, handcuffed him and placed him in the rear of their squad car as they explained the legal conditions he was now under. I was glad they did that, but nothing could make him understand the severity of the damage he had done to me. My mother did not pursue a permanent restraining order against my demands.

A small piece of me still felt bad for him. But that wasn't the end.

Chapter 26:

D.N.A.

"I feel responsible because I never did anything to stop it and just continued to take it over and over and over…"

IN MY EARLY ADULTHOOD, I BEGAN TO research the study of my family's lineage. Because of my interest in history, I wanted to find out if I had any family members who fought in the Civil War. There were a few trips to the library downtown, letters written, phone calls made. I began to learn that the oral history that my grandparents told me was not as accurate as they believed. I saw the commercials for Ancestry.com but never investigated that. Later I moved onto other interests. When I accepted what happened to me and began to explore my childhood, my sister and I began to speak about things that were never discussed before for the very first time.

When my sister and I were young, my mother's company used to have an annual work picnic at *White Swan Amusement Park,* a local amusement park just outside the city. This was a great day for a little boy. Rides, candy, games, fun… and my father never came to these events. That is still very odd to me even today. My wife and I attend everything we can together. Rarely do we go alone, and it would only be due a work schedule or special commitment. My father never came to anything we were involved in and never, ever to my mother's work picnic.

I remember one picnic at the small amusement park. There were all kind of games for the kids, beautiful day and we could ride everything we wanted without any limit. One game involved finding painted stones in a large field and then you could turn them in for money. I found a few but the gold and silver ones are worth the most, silver dollars. I didn't find many of those. I had the ones worth dimes and nickels. One man there, one of my mother's bosses, still gave me silver dollars and it was the way he did it made it unforgettable to me. He came up to me, put them in my palm and squeezed them in my little hand. The experience was very awkward and confusing which made it so memorable to me.

As the layers of events of our childhood began to be peeled back, my sister and I began our discussion.

She told me how she watched our father throw a glass at our mother cutting her arm and how she helped with the bandages on my mother's arm. That she kept a packed bag hidden in her closet in case we had to leave in an emergency and that she had a special hiding place in her closet to go when she was scared.

My sister had often heard the screaming arguments too, specifically ones about "*cheating and affairs.*" That made me remember finding a paperback book hidden once with a title something about "work place affairs." My sister said that she and our mother had left more than once after I was gone.

One thing that really alarmed me was something my sister told me about our grandmother. My sister told me that our grandmother said to her once that she "*wasn't a 'Lucot.'*" I vaguely remember that, but I thought she meant that my sister was more like my mother, not actually genetically different.

The "*secret*" of the physical violence was the one we all kept, hid, protected and lied about but I had another one, a bigger one that I kept all my life. Over the days and weeks, the phone calls and texts we discussed confirmed many of these disturbing memories.

Then my sister asked me a direct question, a chilling question, a piercing question.

"Do you think Dad is my father?"

"No........ I never did." I slowly responded.

It was that simple, all the stress and silence, all the years of secrecy and shame began to lift, evaporating away. This weight I carried was gone and then I began to learn how much my sister examined it.

She responded, *"I don't look like anyone else. I am taller than everyone,"* and it progressed. My sister had calculated a date of conception which would have been the July 4th weekend and it was becoming obvious to me how much time she had spent reviewing and hypothesizing. She felt that our father (*my father*) must have been *"drinking and forced himself"* upon our mother.

Wow, as shocking to me as that statement was, it was not inconceivable at all, it was shocking because someone else <u>knew</u> too. I was not alone with this knowledge and these questions anymore. Although my father was not a "drinker" anything could be possible, but I doubted my sister's hypothesis.

She asked me if I knew who her father might be? *"No, I don't know that."* My sister began to describe her theory to me and as I listened and followed her trail of memories, how she was tying small ideas together, I started thinking of the man with the silver dollars. She told me once our mother took her *"to play"* at a man's house. I said the man's name out loud. She was quiet for a few seconds and confirmed it.

We had the same conclusion.

The fall-out of that discussion involved confronting our mother about this, which I knew she would deny, fluff off and change the subject. The next option was my sister requesting me to get my D.N.A. analyzed and then she could compare it to hers.

Unfortunately, I know I am his biological son. Sometimes when I cough I can hear him or when I see myself at certain angles in a mirror, I see him. When I am working with my hands and they are dirty, I see his hands. So, biologically I must accept that.

Months later, I was attempting to work out an acceptance of a relationship with my mother that included her divorcing her husband and being involved with my family. While having discussions with her about this possibility, I became very frustrated and impatient with her minimization and/or denial of what he did to me and all of us. She continued to refuse to validate the abuses and pain he inflicted, and she began to defend him.

I confronted her about my sister's parentage. It became heated, elevated and I was trying to "shock" her into reality. My focus was not on my sister's father, but on the fact that I didn't care anymore who did what or said what. I didn't care about blame anymore.

I said, *"I don't care if you had 50 affairs!"*

She looked at me with a predetermined expression, *"What?"*

I said, *"Your husband screamed at me about how a wife of a man you had an affair with called him and told him all about it."*

She immediately went into the routine of minimization and physically walking away from me, *"That's silly,"* and *"He doesn't know what he is saying."*

That made me more elevated and angrier. I continued on, *"NO! Why do I have to listen to this and you don't?? Just tell the truth!"*

What came out next made my sister mad at me, but I was tired of playing games and dealing with them both.

"You wonder why Sarah doesn't trust anyone!!!?? Why neither of us trust anyone!!!?? **Why don't you just tell her who her father is?!!"**

Looking back, it was not my question to ask and coincidentally, I advised my sister not to confront our mother at all and now I did it. I *"outed"* her issue. My fuse was so short at that time and desire at any kind of solution was lessening by the day.

My mother responded, I know she was talking but she wasn't *saying anything*. I was looking directly at her, but the one thing that emerged from it was that she never denied it. Any of it.

Periodically through this whole process I will have memories or questions that I try to confirm, and I have contacted our former neighbors, Julie and Natalie Knight. Both have helped me immensely and with many specifics, they are the only people that could do so. I will forever be indebted to them.

While investigating a memory I had about their Dad I asked Natalie if she knew anything about affairs or what my father claimed. I told her that I never thought my father was my sister's father.

Her answer was quick, direct and exact. Just like, "How many inches in a foot?" She blurted out a name, identical to the name I had in my head, the man who I always thought.

It was the name of my mother's co-worker, the "*silver dollar man.*"

Chapter 27:

CHRISTMAS

"She always protected him over us. Always"

THE *"CHRISTMAS SPIRIT"* IS NOT A FEELING that I know. That time of year always was bad, high stress and fighting. We had no traditions and the entire holiday was just one disappointment after another. On Christmas morning, my father never got out of bed to watch us open presents. My mother tried to make that into an occasion that one would expect it to be but that never existed. There are no pleasant memories, none. We never decorated the tree together, never exchanged gifts, decorations were sparse, stress and fights lace every thought and memory I have.

My Grandfather dressed as Santa when I was a boy and later my father would too. It was hell, he would complain and be miserable as I helped him into the costume, wig and beard. Complaining and swearing after having to be begged to do it. But, when he is with his friends in his neighborhood he is the happiest, jovial, generous Santa ever. Just the opposite for us.

My wife and I worked hard to create the opposite. We always go to the tree farm together, hot chocolate, the holiday music, many decorations both inside and out, ornaments from all our travels and vacations. We had electric trains and trollies for our children, visited Santa at his house every year, lights and tours, parties and activities. Cookies next to the fireplace, Santa footprints in the fireplace ashes, *reindeer food* on the porch. I would even go out when there was snow and make *"reindeer footprints"* in the yard.

The Christmas of 2016 found us at our home. The tradition we created was church and dinner on Christmas Eve. My children begged me to invite my mother against my wishes, my experience and my judgement. I had totally separated from my father two years before. My mother came with us for a period of weeks, but went back to him where she currently was living. I did not trust her, she had lied to me about their situation, minimized my wishes and acted like she did not understand others. I relented. My children wanted their grandmother with them.

My mother met us for church and dinner and stayed at our home for Christmas. My father was completely out of our lives, banned from my home, no phone calls, no anything. He knew the severity because I was very clear when I addressed it with him in language and volume that he understands.

On Christmas morning very early, we had coffee and hot chocolate, Christmas carols playing, and we opened presents one-by-one around a beautiful, live blue spruce that we picked and decorated together. My sister was visiting from her home in Colorado, so it was the six of us. I tried to enjoy it, but inside I was not at peace with the situation at all. After all those festivities and a very ornate breakfast I went upstairs to take a nap about noon.

Everything would change drastically after that.

"Dad, Grandpa's here..." my son whispered to me as he awakened me. I got up in shock, thoughts flying all through my head. I thought/hoped he was just here for her and they would leave. I stayed upstairs but my son came right back.

"He is downstairs yelling...."

I went downstairs and was in control for probably a minute. He attacked me with his usual script of how I was *"Never a man!"* and he *"wanted (HIS) family back!"* I instructed everyone upstairs. My wife was behind me in the family room, my sister was positioned between my father and me and my mother was sitting on the stairs with my children. When I looked over at the staircase I could see my mother crying more than anyone and I pointed directly at her and yelled, *"THIS IS YOUR FAULT!!! YOU DID THIS!!!"*

I knew she was lying about her communication with him and it was all crashing down in front of her. My father was still screaming at me. I instructed my son to call 911 and for everyone else to get upstairs.

I then turned to my father directly and kept repeating *"You need to leave. You are not allowed here."* My sister was moving herself to stay positioned between my father and me.

Then I began to taunt him. *"What are you going to do now tough guy!?"*

He switched his attack focusing on how he is sick and his suicidal ideations, *"I just wish I was dead"* and *"You all want me dead"* to which I responded, *"Why don't you do it instead of talking about it all of time you coward!"*

I called him a *"fraud,"* a *"hypocrite,"* and a *"phony,"* and told him that I was, *"one hundred times the man,"* he was.

Then he started pushing my sister. It was then I violently grabbed him and forcibly threw him out of my house, off the porch into my yard. He kept yelling and threatened me, *"Stay away from my mother's grave! She is MY Mother!"*

Within minutes, there were four police vehicles in front of my house on *Christmas Day*. I begged them to take him away and remove the cars in front of my house. The police were very professional, but too tolerant of him. Gradually, they left him leave on his own recognizance and asked me how I wanted to proceed.

I wanted him arrested. He forced himself into my home and threatened me and my mother! I filed formal criminal charges. There was no going back now, and I was not going to erase this for him like everyone else has for decades.

Back inside my home, I found my mother crying in my living room, my wife was in total control, my son said he was okay. My daughter was in her room crying. She was scared and upset. I knew exactly how that felt. I held her, and we talked. I tried to do for her, everything that was never done for me. I told her how much I loved her and how that is not **our** "family" is and how my parents conduct themselves is not how we treat each other. I assured her that this would never ever happen again. After a few questions and she explained to me she was okay, but didn't like how I had to *"throw him into the yard."* I just told her that it had to come to an end and that was the fastest way that I could accomplish that.

My sister was in a bedroom alone. As I walked back downstairs, my mother was still crying loudly in the living room.

By then everyone was in the family room watching a Christmas show on television. I walked up to my mother, she was pleading with me, *"I'm sorry, I'm sorry, "I am just trying to do what is best for everyone,"* she kept repeating.

I asked, *"For who? Who exactly are you trying to best for?"* I received no answers for any of these questions. *"What did you tell him? Did you know he was coming here?"* I showered her with questions.

Her responses were a collection of lies on top of lies and I knew that none of her answers would benefit me. *"I just try to do what's best for everybody else," "I love you."* she avoided all my questions with these statements.

I continued, *"You love me? Exactly HOW do you love me??!! By continually causing pain and stress in my life? How do you love me by lying to me over and over? Exactly how do you love me?"*

Of course, I knew I would not get an answer nor did she even try. I couldn't stop myself.

"You try to do what is best for everyone else? This is the angle you are going to play now? What exactly are you doing for everyone else? You knew your husband was or, at least, might come here today. How exactly did that help me? My wife is battling a cancer diagnosis and stress in the number one enemy right now, how did that help her? I am trying to create a Christmas experience for those two children in there and their Grandmother is crying alone in another room drawing more attention to herself and the

*problem. EXACTLY how is that helping them!!!??? **PLEASE EXPLAIN TO ME HOW YOU ARE DOING WHAT IS BEST FOR EVERYONE ELSE???!!!"***

I was heated and, on a roll, but more so, I was right.

"YOU are doing what is best for everyone??!!!?"

*"In case you haven't noticed my sister trusts no one and has the same issues I do, and <u>you</u> want to do what is best? You want to do something to help her!!? How about tell her who her father is!!! How about that? Then maybe, just maybe she can begin her life with some fragment of the truth. How do you expect us to have any ability to have a relationship?! **TELL HER WHO HER FATHER IS!***

Now, I have to go in there with a smile on my face and try to normalize something out of this day for my children. That is 'DOING WHAT IS BEST' for them. I suggest you try it!!!"

She looked at me and meekly said *"Jimmy, he is sick."*

I couldn't believe it, she was making excuses for him again.

I said, *"You are still going to make excuses for him and defend him!? **REALLY!? You are defending him after what he just did in my house, in front of my children!? There weren't enough police cars here? You are going to sit here and defend him AGAIN!!!"***

I walked out of the room and left her there. Everything was on the surface now and her pathetic attempt to lure me in and manipulate me like she did when I was a child was just sad. She was just as delusional as he was, and I knew I was finished with them both. She would never respect any boundaries that I had to set as a safety concern for my wife and children, aside from the emotional boundaries I required.

A few minutes went by and she walked into the living room where we all were. Her fake demeanor and act that I had seen so many times as a boy made me even angrier. As I began to process everything that happened, I realized she was the focus of my father, his number one reason for coming to my home was because he knew she would be there. The only way he knew that was that my mother told him so. It became very evident that she had to leave. I could not continue having his fixation and target under my roof with me wife and children.

I told her she had to leave.

When the police were questioning me they asked, *"Does he have access to firearms?"*

"Yes" I responded. *"I have seen firearms in his house and I know that several of his friends have weapons that he has borrowed before."*

The officer asked, *"Has he ever had any suicide attempts?"*

"No, but he threatens about it all the time, talks about it passively and actively."

I told them that he was a perfect candidate for *"suicide-by-cop"* and that he is capable of anything and can be extremely dangerous. Pleaded with them to be very careful if they must go to his house.

I have been trained and licensed to carry a concealed firearm solely because of his previous actions and I began to do just that. I was not afraid of him unarmed, but in the event that he might take it to that level, I had to be prepared.

The police officer asked me if I had a firearm and I told him that I did. He asked where I kept it and I told him. The officer responded, *"Well, it's not going to do you any good there."* I understood the severity of his message and advice very clearly and I acted on it.

The next day, I had to go to the police station and complete the paperwork to formally charge him with criminal trespassing and terroristic threats. Then I attained a temporary restraining order as well until I could make it permanent.

Chapter 28:

THE SEARCH

"I know that I am a different person than I was meant to be, born to be"

FOR A FEW YEARS, MY FAMILY HAD A ROUtine where we would meet my mother and wife for lunch after work on Saturdays. Later after my son began to drive, this tradition continued and sometimes I would have other things going on, but I was always invited.

After my mother went back to her husband, she organized and attempted to have lunch with my children on a Saturday afternoon without inviting me. This was a **"secret lunch"** from me. When I confronted her about it, of course it was denial. I was not going to allow her to start her indoctrination of my children. I had previously given her three conditions for her to be involved in my, and my children's lives:

- 1. Admit to the events of the past and her role in them.
- 2. Have a complete three-year Protection from Abuse order against her husband.
- 3. No contact with her husband at all.

I did this as a safety issues, to protect my family and children. She failed at all three and showed no interest in my wishes and thus seeing my children, who her only grandchildren.

I asked her that if she were to actually leave her husband to please not lease an apartment in the town I live in. My sole reason? Because I knew he would go after her and that my name would end up in the newspaper embarrassing my wife, myself and our family.

I clearly instructed her to not contact my friends as she had done in the past.

Only a few weeks had past and multiple friends began to let me know that my parents were contacting them "*to talk.*"

One friend told me that my mother stated this to her about me; "*I don't know what I did wrong? I went all of his games.*" Another family friend said my mother claimed that my father had "*a brain accident from a past surgery* (and that) *was the reason for his behavior.*" I attended all of my father's surgeries, met with his physicians and closely reviewed his conditions. My mother fabricated the "*brain accident*" completely.

I confronted my mother about what she knew and when did she know it. She said that she "*couldn't take sides,*" and that I "*couldn't just give up on him,*" because "*he is all alone now.*" She denied everything.

I named names of people she called, made claims to and contacted. She stated that they are "*all lying*" and that she "*did not contact anyone.*" I asked who her therapist was that she claimed she was going to and she could not state any specific name, location, diagnosis, licensure or type of therapy she was supposedly participating in.

She said that she was not in contact with her husband and was in fact, attaining a Protection from Abuse (P.F.A.) order.

I asked her one final time if she was contacting my friends and she lied to me.

My response?

"*Do not ever contact me or any of my family again in any way,*" and I hung up.

Sure, enough his actions at my home on Christmas Day were in fact in the "Court" section of our local newspaper:

"James D. Lucot, 74, of Pittsburgh waived to court charges of defiant trespass and harassment (two counts) filed Jan. 10 by Cranberry Township Police."

Chapter 29:

TWO MEN AND A JUDGE

"I know that I was born good and innocent".

AFTER I WENT TO THE LOCAL POLICE DEPART-
ment and completed all the paperwork and officially filed the
charges, I had to wait for the actual court date. I wanted none
of it in my life anymore, but I was not going to allow it to
continue. I called almost daily until I received the court date.

The victim's advocate for the court contacted me to
explain the procedure and if I had any questions. She was
extremely professional, sympathetic and supportive. I had
to take a day off work, and I went alone.

The local magistrate was a former policeman and the
father of one of my former football players. We knew each
other well. I went to his office early and asked to see him. I
told him how embarrassed and humiliated I was, and he
assured me of how common this was. He was very respectful
and understanding, but I was still extremely embarrassed
and ashamed. I requested that this hearing be sealed from
the media since I did not want his name (my name) in the
newspaper since I was a teacher and my wife was a psychiatrist with her private practice a mile away. He was genuinely
nice to me, but could not guarantee that. He smiled at me and
said, *"Jim, you know we have a thing called the U.S. Constitution
here and freedom of the press, but I will try."*

I sat down and waited.

The lawyer for the county was very supportive as well. He asked if I thought he would bring legal representation which I knew he would not since he likes his money way too much and would never pay an attorney.

"Do you think he will bring anyone with him?" he asked me next. That thought became very stressful to me, just imagining who might be coming. He had many acquaintances that were not strangers to the legal system and I knew all of them. Some of them I met and interviewed recently. They knew and supported me and were surprisingly open with me. I began to guess who he might bring.

Gradually, the police officers and court officials all began entering the court room that was very new, clean and modern. One told me that my father was outside in the waiting room. A court official told me he brought *"two men with him."* Finally, my father came in dressed in shabby clothes with hair balding, unkept, stringy and long. He was "extra" disheveled and after I saw his "performance" his appearance fit the role.

I wondered who he would bring with him. I knew he was a coward, a hypocrite and didn't have the guts to walk in there alone. Like I did. He had a crew of questionable personalities to pick from. All of his friends, those men knew me, who I was, some for my entire life. I thought of so many guys he may have brought, I knew he would not have an attorney because he would not pay for that.

I had never seen either of these men before. Big guys in their sixties, one had a t-shirt on with *"McKees Rocks"* written on it. That was a town next to the neighborhood I grew up notorious for its high crime reputation. This was the same area were my mother wanted me to go and find her niece. The two men accompanying my father looked like they might have been bikers trying not to look like bikers. These two thugs just stared at me the entire time in between whispering to him as they sat less than 10-feet from me in the same row. I guess they were there to intimidate me, but the effect on me was just the opposite. I realized that any of his old friends that actually knew me wouldn't come with him, or he was too embarrassed to ask or tell them where he was going and exactly who it was that was going to be testifying against him. That became very validating to me, that he would not ask or inform the men who actually knew me about this or bring them as his escorts. That he understood that they might not attend if it was me. He was ashamed and embarrassed and did not want them to know what he did to me and my family.

Later, I talked to two of his old friends that knew me (who did not accompany him to court that day) and that was exactly what they told me. That they never were comfortable how he treated my mother in public nor the situations that he had put me in. They both realized that and cut off contact with him because of it.

The proceedings began, the court officials read the events, charges and legal possible outcomes. I just needed to be there to confirm that I was committed to pressing charges and was not going to drop them at a later date as many victims of domestic violence do. The magistrate instructed my father to approach the bench and swore him in.

Now, if you ever saw the mafia boss, Vincent *"The Chin"* Gigante of the Genovese Crime Family in New York, who I know my father watched on television, my father was imitating him exactly. My father loved those type of shows. Vincent Gigante was also known as *"The Odd father"* because he acted senile in an attempt to stay out of jail by walking around Brooklyn in a robe feigning mental illness by talking to telephone poles and himself while he knew he was being watched by the F.B.I.

My father jumbled papers, acted like he didn't understand the questions and just made unattached statements such as, *"I am not sure why I am here,"* *"I don't know what I did to make my son hate me so much,"* *"I am just broken hearted,"* and repeating *"What does that mean?"*

But the magistrate would have none of it and became stricter with his antics. He forced my father to clearly answer him and even made him repeat his instructions back to him. Then my father claimed to be going for *"mental health treatment."* He stated, *"I am in therapy and seeing a psychiatrist, I am just trying to do what everyone wants me to do..."* but of course he had no proof of this. (A few days later my mother will make this same claim almost word for word although she supposedly had no contact with him what so ever. How could she know that?)

He only does what he wants, and there is no one who denies mental health as remotely legitimate as him. He would never admit he had any problem at all aside from a *"mental health"* problem. No way.

The magistrate asked my father if he accepted the charges or would plead not guilty and proceed to Criminal Court. My father turned and looked at his two new "associates" seated 10-feet behind him. *"No"*, he answered.

Immediately the magistrate stated, *"You do not accept these charges? You will appear at the stated date at the Butler County Courthouse."* That was it. They read the court date, ordered a $10,000 bond and dismissed him.

I walked directly at his two *"friends"* and passed them as close to them as I could, brushing the leg of one of them. I wasn't a little boy anymore.

The three of them left the court room and the door closed behind them. The lawyer looked at me with a disparaging grin and said, *"I think he needs to have a taste of criminal court."*

The magistrate explained to me that his case would now progress to the county criminal court and that my father had no idea what he was doing. He asked me if my father would attain a lawyer for his own defense. *"No way, he is so tight he would never pay that"*, I replied.

The court lawyer said if he *"goes up there unrepresented he will have no chance."*

That court date came up weeks later and I attended that trial, although I was not required to as the victim. Another day off from work, and I found myself in a waiting room with children, pieces of families, small children playing around my feet as I sat at the table, in a suit and tie reading a book. The victim advocate came to me and gave me some instructions, she was so nice and then the court appointed attorney for me, as the victim, sat down with me as well.

We had spoken before so there, were no new issues. **Then my mother walked in.** I had no idea she would be there; the court scheduled our hearings back to back. We sat for a half hour or more without a word. I was angry, I wanted nothing to do with either of their lives and their lies.

The same victim's attorney then sat down with her just across from me. I could hear their whole conversation. My mother immediately began minimizing the facts. Then I heard her request. My mother asked the court for a three-month P.F.A.! Previously I told her if she wanted to see my children she must attain a three-year protection from abuse order against her husband as a safety measure.

I walked across that waiting room, *"WHAT?! What are you doing?"*

She asked the court for a three-month protection from abuse order pending he receives *"mental health treatment."*

Wow! I just heard that same phrase a few weeks prior. Now, I knew they were in contact after she told me they were not. I knew she was lying to me and my sister, and lying to the court. I told the victim's attorney this and she was very experienced and immediately realized that my mother was not reliable. I am sure she has seen many wives go this far only to drop all the charges.

She asked my mother directly, *"Did he ever hit you?"* My mother responded very slowly and calculated, *"no."*

I interjected loudly, *"She is lying! Show them the scars Mom! Show her the scars on your arm where he threw you through the wall! Where he broke the glass on your arm! Show her Mom!"* The attorney looked at me and slightly shook her head negatively sideways. My mother was lying to court appointed lawyer and the assistant district attorney.

My hearing was first. These proceedings were very direct, cold and mechanical. Very different from the magistrate hearing. The judge was authoritarian and there was no small talk.

He asked my father, *"Did you ever hit your wife?"* He answered meekly, *"No, no I never did that."* Now, he was lying under oath.

I was sitting directly behind him. The judge read the charges, found him guilty of defiant trespass and two counts of harassment, fined him and ordered a three-year P.F.A. against him — including my and my wife's workplaces and my children's schools — fined him and said, ***"Do you understand that if you contact the victim in any way you will be in a cell? <u>You will be on a cot</u>, Mr. Lucot. Do you understand that?"***

That concluded my case and they asked me if I had any questions. I asked if I had to stay any longer and when I was informed that I did not, I walked out leaving my parents in court for my mother's P.F.A. hearing.

My sister also filed charges in the state she lives in and attained the maximum three-year P.F.A. there as well. I will renew the P.F.A. in three years and continue to do so as long as he is still alive.

Chapter 30:

INVALIDATION

"It is a cruel disappointment to a child when parents do not act like they should. I did my part, they did not do theirs."

PRIOR TO ALL THESE CONFRONTATIONS AND before I set any boundaries at all, several of my students from recent years planned a large surprise birthday party, with the assistance of my wife and children, at my home. This was also to celebrate my nomination as Pennsylvania Teacher of the Year. My sister was the one assigned to get me away from home and be the decoy. We went to lunch and then she told me we were going to our parent's house *"to discuss a living will."*

Needless to say, I did not want to go there or do that at all, but I began to realize there was a surprise party for me of some type, so I played along. Next, I found myself in my parent's house sitting at their dining room table across from my father, on my birthday.

He started baiting me with unrelated topics such as politics or racial issues neither of which I would involve myself in. Laughing and joking. My mother and sister were facing the kitchen and my father looked at me, directly, eye-to-eye. He quickly and slightly hidden from anyone else in the room, he gave me "the finger" so only I could see him. This is what he was reduced to, on my birthday, knowing that in a few minutes there would be a huge surprise party for me given by my students and family, with friends and former students and football players. Knowing all of that, my father decided to tell me to f*** myself. He had to control and sabotage everything, but it was no longer working with me. His normal tactics were no longer having the same impact and he knew it.

Thinking back, I remembered my wife and I celebrated one of our wedding anniversaries as a family by going downtown to a nice dinner and a Pirates game. We always included my mother with the four of us and she would sleep over at our house. She called me the morning of that game and said she *"didn't think it was best"* that she slept over because she was *"afraid"* my father might come. I interpreted this as honest, but I wonder if that even happened or was it just her mechanism to get the focus and attention on her.

After she returned to him, she finally was permitted to buy a new car, and she brought it to my house. I went outside and told her it was nice, but it was hollow since this was after she left living with us and went back to him. She responded to me, *"I am so happy because you are being nice to me."*

When I explained to my sister that my mother was no longer permitted in my home or with my children she said, *"You can't do that. Finally, Mom is doing everything we always wanted by leaving him and she needs our support now more than ever."* She pleaded to me.

I yelled, ***"No! Where was she when we needed her support our whole lives and never got it? She looked out for herself and we paid the price. She needs to support us both then and now!!!"***

My sister and I have never spoke about it again. I disagree. My mother's manipulation tactics are still in effect with my sister. She will ride both sides of the fence clinging to some hope for something that never existed all while still being swayed by our mother that she is the victim, and she that needs our help and support.

I can see how my father always was in total denial of everything and he pivots immediately from his responsibility for the abuse he delivered upon us to my mother's affair. He told me endless times that I will *"never be a man,"* and now, I can understand today that I wasn't raised by one. I became a man solely on my own and he is still the coward that abuses women and children. He is a thief and a fraud.

Every day that passes without my mother making any attempt to see her grandchildren, validates me. The bottom line is that our mother always chose him first over my sister and I, now even above my children, her only grandchildren. She always did then and still does today.

Chapter 31:

MY LIFE TODAY

"So many things I am doing now is for the very first time in my life."

MANY THINGS HAVE BECOME CLEARER TO me and is very difficult to accept that I couldn't or didn't realize it then. I find that extremely frustrating. I know that I lived in a constant state of conflict, my parents were always in different stages of arguments, fights and grudges with other family members, neighbors, co-workers and mostly each other. Too many of these situations led to confrontations that brewed and progressed, it didn't matter if I was around or not it because everything was discussed always went down right in front of me.

Almost every morning, I awake with what I have labeled a *"mental hangover."* If I had any dreams I have to review them and process them. I try to minimize this time period, I try to reframe the negative memories or triggers into what is real and how my life is today. There is almost always a sadness or unhappiness connected someway so I try to consciously focus on the positives in my life every morning. Some days it is an insurmountable force just to get up and begin something which I gradually will, but I will also repeat that same process the next day over again.

I have a *"bargaining"* process that I go through in the morning where I debate how difficult things might be and how I can make excuses to get out of them. I then look forward to when the day is over and all of the tasks I have to do that day are completed and then I can return to my bed. I still have hard times, but I try to make one good day and follow it up with another, *"to put two good days together."*

I am much more empathetic and less judgmental of people than I use to be. I am very proud of the life and family my wife and I have made for ourselves. That is my main motivation for everything that I do. I will always be committed to this issue and bringing awareness of these abuses.

I hope today with social media and most of all, education and knowledge that these situations can be identified, interventions be made, support and protections be placed, and prevention will be the immediate action so that no child will have to be subjected to anything less than they deserve: a loving, nurturing and safe environment where they know they are always cared for and protected. That no little boy or girl has to feel like they are the only person in the world like themselves. Like I did for so long.

One of my former students and I had lunch recently. She goes to the University of San Francisco and we have stayed close throughout her collegiate life. She was describing her roommate to me and all the unique things about her. I found one specific aspect, particularly alarming. She told me that this friend decided to change her name. I found that very curious to me, but the more I thought about that I realized that is something I wished I could have done too. My name is the same as my fathers. I am a *"junior."* Sometimes when I hear it aloud it strikes me as someone else, not mine, just words that I have no connection to.

This sensation extends into my life in other ways. I physically look like him, there are many easily recognizable features that are more than similar. Often, I will see my reflection in a car window or a mirror and *"see"* him. Quickly, I look away and try to eliminate my conscious awareness, to erase the entire experience.

135

Another eerie perception that occurs much too frequently is when I am driving with my family or taking my daughter somewhere, we will be laughing or joking and suddenly I will look at my hands on the steering wheel and see his hands. Like they are not mine, not connected to me. I don't like these occurrences and they make me uncomfortable and piercing. I try to drive *"underhanded"* with my hands on the bottom of the steering wheel because of that. Everything changes inside of me, negative and dark, sad and angry. I am looking at my hands on this keyboard and I can see his hands right now.

I have and continue to participate in multiple negative thinking, PTSD, child abuse and depression studies at the University of Pittsburgh. Many times, in some of the study scenarios, visuals and interview questions are quite disturbing. One researcher stopped the question progression asked me if he could ask me a *"non-study question?"* *"Sure"*, I responded. He focused and slowly inquired, *"Why do you do this?"* That answer came to me very simply. *"Because I need to feel that something good can come out of this. It validates me. It helps me to know that all this really happened."*

Two years after I banned my father from all aspects of my family, I was working in my garage and my son walked up to me with a very serious look on his face. He said *"Dad, … Grandpap just called me."* He called my son's cell phone the night before he was leaving for his freshman year of college. The night before we would drive him eight hours away from home for the first time. The night before my wife and I, like so many families, would move our child into a dorm room, take him to dinner, buy him supplies and drive away in silence as we entered the next stage of our lives. My father decided to call my son that night, once again in a futile attempt to draw the attention to himself and upset everyone. To sabotage the joy felt by others, joy that he could never feel.

I immediately called my mother who began to rationalize his behavior and *"that (I) have to understand (he) was sick."* She denied it was him, *"How could (he) do that? (he) doesn't even have that phone number."* She acted like was no issue at all and everything was all going to go away. That someday we would all unite together in a utopian Norman Rockwell-like setting. I clearly and specifically directed her to delete all my numbers from his phone and for him to, *"never contact any of my family in any way. Not on the phone, not the mail or not a smoke signal!"* I made her repeat it back to me. A few months later, I would be saying the same exact thing to her.

This past Christmas (2017) my father violated the P.F.A. by sending me a handwritten letter stating how my grandparents, aunts, uncles hate me. He sent this to me one year following his Christmas "appearance" at my home. He did not sign it and mailed it without a return address. All of the relatives listed were dead. The list of names was followed by *"HATE YOU."* He wrote this in his very distinct Catholic school cursive that is reminiscent of an elementary school age child. Only he would know the names of these individuals. My sister felt that he sent the letter as an excuse to see me. I not only disagree with that, I can't even imagine him conspiring to write that letter for that purpose. He knew what he was doing and why. My father wanted to hurt me anyway he can and make me pay for his perceived offenses against him. Even more hurtful is that I let my daughter open it. She likes opening mail and she was opening Christmas cards and got to that envelope. She asked me oddly, *"Dad, what is this?"* I quickly took it out of her hands, *"Oh, that's silly junk mail honey".*

This resulted in another court date where I had to appear again to testify. These incidents are a reminder and trigger to my abusive past at his hands. I will continue to act until he finally is imprisoned or dies.

While I was in the "victim's waiting room" at the Butler County Courthouse speaking to the Assistant District Attorney. I was trying to explain the psychological games my father plays with me like this letter. At the exact same moment, I could see him out in the hallway standing like a gunfighter ready to draw trying to intimidate me. My father was staring at me through the open door after he was warned to have no contact with me. I whispered to the Assistant D.A., *"turn around"* and he saw my father in this sad *"want to be tough guy pose"* glaring at me. The D.A. quickly stood up and loudly ordered the bailiff to remove my father from the hallway immediately and warn him.

The D.A. told me my father claimed that he *"could not recall if (he) wrote the letter"* and my mother lied to back him up. She said she *"could not confirm it was my father's handwriting."* The D.A. threatened to take them in courtroom under oath and then they agreed to extend his probation six more months.

Shortly after that I received an embarrassing phone call from a very close friend. *"Jimmy, I don't how to tell you this, but your mom is trying to friend me on Facebook and I don't know what to do."* I apologized and asked her to send me a screen shot of it, which I forwarded to my father's probation officer. That is the last contact I have had.

Routinely, various people and distant relatives will bring their names up to me and I immediately respond, *"I have no contact with them and they are legally barred from contacting me."* Upon each instance of these occurrences I receive shock and apologies, so they obviously are not receiving the same information when they speak to my parents.

I currently do not have any of their contact information nor do I want it. Throughout my life my father told me many times his wishes at the time of his death. I heard the same lecture over and over my whole life usually with how he will also be haunting me. If I am contacted and/or am responsible for those decisions solely based on our genetics, I will honor his wishes. No funeral, a pine box and I will not attend any of it. I assume my sister will handle our mother's planning. I won't be attending that either.

Trust. My best friend told me this once. I was dating a girl and I told him I was going to break up with her. He said, *"Man, I would hate to date you. You don't trust anyone."* Another friend made a joke about me and said, *"Let's list everyone Jimmy respects. Dennis Wayne (my football coach). That's it."* I respected extremely few and trusted none. It is still extremely difficult, but I am much closer to being able to trust than ever in my life now. My wife has helped me immensely and is extremely understanding and insightful but still I have to consciously remind myself of that fact.

Forgiveness. I have found that there a many opinions and theories regarding the need to forgive, etc. Here are my thoughts. You cannot forgive anyone who does not honestly ask for forgiveness. No one is **deserving** of forgiveness. If someone is not sincerely sorry for their actions and offenses, if they want to debate or bargain for forgiveness, it is inauthentic and will just end up delaying your progress and/or hurting you more. There is absolutely no gray area, either they admit and accept everything they have done without any conditions or there is no forgiveness. A "deathbed" is not the environment of a sincere apology nor true sorrow or an environment to request for my forgiveness.

Confrontation. I have found that attempting to confront an abuser, enabler, a narcissist, etc. probably will just repeat the same behaviors that resulted in the reasons for the confrontation in the first place. It will not be worth your effort, emotions and time. If the individual is receptive to accepting responsibility and discussion, then this may be effective, but I have not had this experience in my situation. When I first set small boundaries, they were immediately and completely not honored, minimized and disparaged.

Boundaries. There are no conditions on happiness. It is not a "condition" of something or someone else. *"I will be happy when..."* or *"I will be happy if"* he or she is with me. The same is for boundaries. If one sets a boundary to protect themselves emotionally, psychologically or physically and an individual has any condition upon it then they are part of the problem too. There are no conditions when healthy boundaries are set. They may be altered in time, but that is up to you. All of one's boundaries must be honored completely without any condition or *"gray area."*

I have one continuous regret throughout my life and that has been reinforced to me throughout this process. I wish I was stronger and more knowledgeable then so that I could have protected my sister or rescued her. When I reached high school and college I could drive, and that opened more places that I could control. Again, I felt sadness and despair over leaving my sister behind. There were times I was escaping, but couldn't take her with me. I think about those times often and desire a different outcome, one that made me older and more capable, so that I could have changed her outcome.

She and our mother had a very different relationship, they seemed closer or maybe I imagined that to make myself feel better. I assumed it would be different for her and I honestly believed that or convinced myself of that — mostly to make myself feel better. I am haunted to this day that I didn't protect her in some way. I just wrote her a letter yesterday about that. I wish I was stronger back then.

We just got off the phone and one of my answers to her summarizing our lives was, simply that my father was *"a very, very bad man...."*

EPILOUGUE

I AM A HUSBAND, FATHER, TEACHER, PART-time college instructor, Holocaust scholar, mentor, volunteer, woodworker, photographer, writer, former (and possibly future) football coach, friend and now, a lifelong advocate for the abused. I am beginning to accept these things and to finally be able to be proud of my accomplishments and take ownership of them and what occurred that brought me to this point in my life.

That has always been very difficult for me to realize that. This actually was an assignment that I have worked on in therapy. In the course of this exercise, I can see how my father was none of these things for me or for anyone. He has no legacy other than sadness, pain, grief and heartache. He is a predator of the weak and too much of a coward to look inward where the real problem lies. He has alienated children and relatives, life-long friends and neighbors. I can see now that I have made different choices for myself and my family. The choice to accept and recognize this internally was the most challenging and frightening undertaking of my life and I am just beginning to see the other side.

Sometimes I find myself still looking out at my driveway, fearful that his car may be there.

Many times, when I see a small child, happily playing it makes me smile but often I will get sad because I know that was never me.

Recently, my daughter shared with me that she has had nightmares that my father is coming or is outside our house.

We have talked about that and I think that talking is the solution. I am happy that she trusts me enough to share her feelings with me. I never had anything like that, not at her age, not ever. I took out the decorative door with windows on our basement and replaced it with a steel utility door with a large deadbolt lock, so my daughter would not be afraid. I showed her how it locks and still check it every night.

I continue with therapy. I have accepted the fact that I have a chronic diagnosis that has no cure and will require some degree of professional attention for the rest of my life. I explore everything I can about this subject and potential treatments or techniques that can help me. I have identified certain aspects and triggers that I can process and solve on my own, but every day brings new challenges.

Sadness can overwhelm me extremely quickly, sometimes like quicksand. Like a wave, it immediately can cover every facet of my life. Several negative ideas surround me, an emotional state of how I don't fit in a *"throw-away society"* and sometimes I feel that I am too damaged that I can't be corrected. That I am beyond help. I convince myself that I should just stay away from everyone and everything. A constant state of dread and a permanent alertness and fear is always just around the corner if I let it.

I search for faults in myself to justify why I feel depressed, why I feel weak and why I must deserve this in my life. These feelings and thoughts have lessened but continue to surface from time to time without predictability or constraint.

My friend is a yoga instructor and she is truly the only person who could get me to even try it. She has been a beacon of support and hope for me. I also attend yoga weekly, more if I can. I found another instructor who works with veterans with PTSD. She understands me, and I feel safe there. This practice I have discovered to be extremely beneficial as well.

My family is busy with many athletic practices and activities, so we eat out often. Many of these nights we also stop at ice cream and yogurt shops on the way home. We always have, and we all enjoy it. The past issue of *"ice cream"* is one

I have successfully identified and effectively resolved. I still will not order a "cone," but I think that is out of my preference now, rather than fear. The cone is no longer a trigger, but it is still a memory that cannot be unfortunately, like so many others, cannot ever be forgotten.

Many of these places are the employers of my students and it is fun for me to see them outside of school. These appropriate interactions outside the classroom can really impact the students and I like them to meet my family too. I have learned to make these times a positive for my family. I have learned that I have "triggers," recollections or events that remind me of past abuses that cause great stress and pain. These occurrences can and have caused significant discomfort for me and those around me.

These are some issues and problems that I deal with regularly:
- I rarely enjoy anything in actual time.
- When attending events or activities I think about leaving or when the event will be over, so I can go home, but then later I will appreciate it.
- I often feel disconnected from the present.
- Sometimes I have intrusive thoughts (and dreams) – extreme violence, lethal accidents, driving in opposite lane, etc. that are very alarming and disturbing.
- I have accepted that I will never understand what it is like to have a normal interaction or reaction in actual real time.
- It is still hard for me to totally give up hope that the past could have been different for me. I will always be angry about that.
- Everything is completely "black and white" to me which is not effective to progress.
- I have extreme noise sensitivity and am easily startled by any loud noises, especially doors slamming, dogs and sneezes.

- I continue to experience intermittent anxiety attacks, body armoring, nightmares, chronic sleep disturbances, clenched jaws and making fists.
- I don't like crowds and often find myself wanting to isolate.
- I sleep with a radio on all night. Talk radio only. I don't know why but it helps me. I take small radios with me where I travel.
- If I go out somewhere, it helps me if I have an escape, my own vehicle so I know I can control if I want or need to leave.
- I find watching TV shows, news, movies, etc. with any domestic violence or children suffering very unsettling and will change the channel or leave the room.
- I am overprotective of my own children and worry unnecessarily.
- I often have irrational attachments to inanimate objects.
- Sometimes I get very angry at myself for allowing this to happen to me for so long and that I never recognized it and did anything about it.
- I have identified many triggers that can greatly impact me, and I have been able to create solutions to several of these, but periodically a new one will strike me which I perceive as very defeating and upsetting to me. That it will never end.

Now for the successes:
- Therapy (Cognitive Behavior Therapy) has been the number one help to me.
- I have found yoga to be extremely beneficial for me.
- I have tried hypnosis, but that did not produce the desired benefits for me.
- I have completed several child abuse victim, P.T.S.D., depression academic studies at the University of Pittsburgh and I will continue to do this. I find it very validating and it makes me feel like a positive can come from my experiences.

- I found that journaling has been very helpful and rewarding.
- Writing takes considerable time and effort, it had little immediate recognizable gains for me. The long-term effects have produced impressive insights and identifiable issuesthat I could grasp and build from.
- I have followed a pescatarian diet to assist in limiting serotonin levels to lessen CPTSD symptoms. I feel that this has been effective in minimizing the length of perseverating and negative thinking. I also appreciate the discipline and feeling of control that maintaining the diet brings me.
- I have taken up woodworking and I really enjoy spending time working on projects that require long term planning that takes up a lot of my thoughts.
- I also took up photography and have found that this provides me with a socially acceptable "license" to excuse myself and walk away at public events if I become anxious or uncomfortable. I discovered this when I did not have my camera with me and how different my experience was without it.
- I have always enjoyed reading and I continue to do that as well but focus on C/P.T.S.D. related memoirs, studies and articles.
- After being so quiet and keeping secrets all my life, I find talking about what happened to me with others that have had similar backgrounds very comforting. I am fortunate to have several supportive people in my life and many of them have personal histories that are similar. These people's interest and opinions have been helpful to me.
- I have great hope for ketamine to be approved and marketed for treatment of depression and PTSD symptoms in the near future.
- I use PTSD specific essential oils (Orange, bergamot, basil, lemongrass, lavender) in my home and vehicle.

- I am active on social media sites supporting others with abuse histories.
- I try to maintain a complete schedule with little unplanned downtime. Structure and being busy is very effective for me being positive.
- This project, writing this book, became my focus. This did not start out as a "book" just my journal, but it evolved into something that I had to do. My only objective, and possible goal, was that if it could help one person then it would totally be worth it.

Acknowledgements:

I WOULD LIKE TO SINCERELY THANK THE
following:

My wife, Suzanne and our children for their support, patience and understanding. My sister for her sincerity, validation and honesty. I sincerely hope that she will progress to resolve all the damages that were undeservingly inflicted upon her. Eric Jacoby. Darren Schoppe. Gary Dellovade. Alicia Chico. Denise David-Reiling. Sandy Barch. Mrs. Linda Brooks. Bob and Erin Ceh. Bonnie and Dennis Coates. Mrs. Rose Dukovich. Samantha Franks. Vera Marshall. Father Jerry Wilson. Eddie Jones. Larry Bettencourt. Ron Cepek. Mike Short. Jay Junko. Dr. Sal Palumbo, M.D., Leigh Ann Totty. Avi Ben-Hur. Andy and Monica Sieber. Larry and Connie Mosier. Dr. Suzanne Stragand, D.O., Maggie Aebi. Chris Marrucci. Paul Rose. Lily Hope Lucario. Eric Clapton. Ernest Hemingway. Howard Chandler. Jack Sittsamer. Dr. Tsipi Gur. M/Sgt. Abie Abraham. Capt. Vinnie Vicari. Capt. Don Alexander. Col. Jim Dollar. His Holiness, The Dalai Lama. Michael Kuzbel, Michela Sieber and Carson Jacoby. Kathleen Ganster. Isurvive.org. Tomato Pie Café, DeBlasio's, Mineo's, and Rico's Restaurants.

Ron Butschle
Parker Johnston
Mr. and Mrs. Harold White
Bob and Sherry Jacoby

Tim and Kate Fazio
Susan and Josie White
and
Alison Schuster and Shellie Vincent, M.S.W.

APPENDIX

Therapy assignment: *"Write an open letter to your parents"*:
(This is the exact letter I wrote as an assignment for one of my therapy exercises.)
15 MAY 2017
TO: *****

FROM: James D. Lucot JR

RE: You are not worth my time in writing this.

I know I was not born this way.

I know that I was innocent and good and did not deserve what you two did to me.

Your selfish act to have children knowing that your anger, immaturity, selfishness, insincerity, hatred of each other, lack of control and sheer disrespect for me would never provide a safe environment for a child cost me so much pain, sadness, insecurity, hurt, disgust.... there are no words to describe it. None.

Your words:

"You will never be a man!"
"I hope you get a bitch just like I did, you know she's a bitch, don't you?"
"Her mother was a bitch and so is she."
"She ruined my life."
"Drop dead bitch!"
"Go to Hell Bitch!"
"You see what I have to put up with?"
"Last one in is a nigger baby"
"You know that your uncle hits your aunt too?"
"What the hell do you want me to do about it?" (When I told you, I was getting married)
"I am going to come to your house and take a shit on your couch!"

My identity was sacrificed, my childhood was shattered. You two spoke about anything and everything in front of me. You two dumped all your anger, aggravation, stress, unhappiness, disgust in your marriage, hatred of each other, hatred of work, all on me. Because of you, I am not the person I was supposed to be.

I never had a family. I had a lie. I had a dark, evil secret. You made me into a liar, an actor, a fraud, a fake, a poser and you tried to keep me that way. You insulted and said horrible things about the people I cared about like my grandparents and the White family. You are cowards, gutless and spineless for taking it out on me and exposing me to that as a child. I have no other memory.

Why did the Dean of Nursing at Duquesne call you to an appointment? I know she asked you about "your husband." What was her concern? It obviously was about me. I was never told nor was it explained to me.

What did the specialist you took me to tell you about my bedwetting? I know you spoke to Dr. Saul, and my grandparents and Julie and Natalie and whoever else when I begged you not to tell anyone crushing my trust.

What did that doctor say? I know that I stopped bedwetting for weeks and months at a time and it would come back. Why? Stress? Watching him beat you? What did the specialist you took me to say about my hair falling out? You told me it was from wearing a baseball hat too much. Really? It wasn't stress? Really? He teased me in front of Grandpap Lucot and Jackie about my bedwetting. He never once supported me or talked to me about that never once. Nobody did. But <u>you</u> spoke to people about it, didn't you?

I cried alone in my room so many times about that and so many other reasons, pick one. I had so many things to cry about. Your cure? Telling me that I didn't have it so bad, telling me others had it worse or telling how bad my grandmother treated you. You never protected me but asked, demanded that I protect your lies. My needs, my concerns, my health was all sacrificed for yours.

You did the best for <u>you</u>... NOT me.

Your secret was more important than me. I paid for your problems, your weakness, your cowardice, your selfishness. I paid with my innocence, my childhood, my time, my thoughts, my guilt, my everything.

**My life was the casualty for your war with each other.
I am the victim.**

I lost so much time, memories, people, relationships have been impaired or blocked or damaged by what you did to me. I have no idea what a relationship should look like. Television and books were my teachers. The house we lived in was never a home. It was a vacuum of love, nurturing, support, understanding, teaching, learning, sincerity, goodness, help... all sucked away before ever reaching me. All that remained for me was screaming, hatred, ugliness, threats, swearing, insults, blame, meanness, violence, beating, breaking, hiding, lies, silence, suffering, exile, confinement.... nobody came for me and even if they did you would "show" them.

I have a chronic issue with no cure that I will have to address for the rest of my life and fight everyday not to pass the curse you gave me along to my children. Although the fight is hard, the choice is easy because I love my children and I will protect them and do whatever is humanly possible for them never to experience one second of what you did to me. How is the choice to protect a child even a decision?

You are thieves.

You robbed me, you stole from me what isn't yours. Now tell yourselves something different, rationalize it and deny it but you know you are thieves.

There is no forgiveness, you robbed me of that too. I have no faith in a God because there was never a God for me. Where was He for me? How could there even be a God? How on earth would He let me be mistreated like that? Why would He let this happen to me? Why? Because I must be bad. So, you gave that to me too. I must **DESERVE** all of this because I am bad. There was no God for me.

You stole from your employer and who knows who else and made it like you were deserving of this. You surrounded us with convicted felons, drug dealers, pedophiles and had them at our house.

You almost had me convinced too. You almost got away with it, but I stopped it. I have a family and I admit when I am wrong. I will never be like you. I would never let anyone mistreat a child in my presence.

I could write so much more, so many more hurtful and nasty things you said about my relatives, none of which I have any relationship with. You taught me how to hold grudges, talk behind people's backs, how to hate, how to mistreat, how not to take responsibility and blames others, how to threaten and use violence, you taught me exactly what not to do. Now start lying to yourselves, tell yourselves that this didn't happen…

Submitted Victim Impact Statement for Butler County Court:

VICTIM IMPACT STATEMENT

VICTIM: JAMES DENNIS LUCOT JR.

DEFENDANT: *****

C.A. NUMBER: CP-10-0000371-2017

1. The criminal actions of ***** have made my wife and daughter afraid in our own home. I watch them routinely check and re-check our doors and locks multiple times every evening and night. My wife is battling a cancer diagnosis and the additional stress due to his breaking in to my home has created an unhealthy environment for her. She is afraid and scared. I replaced our basement door with a security steel door and deadbolt lock solely on the advice of law enforcement because of his statements, actions and threats. My daughter is thirteen years old and wants to stay home alone at times when we do errands *"like her friends do"*. I will never let her home alone because of his threats and actions.

I check all locks every night in my home. I have found myself checking outside periodically looking at my driveway and then I realize why I am doing it. I find myself looking at the entrance door of the gyms of my daughter's basketball games fearing he will appear. I have dreams about him coming to my house.

***** has contacted my several of my friends both on the phone and in person asking to *"talk"* with them. Then they call me asking what to do about it and are concerned for themselves which is extremely embarrassing to me.

I have had to experience many sad and uncomfortable conversations and discussions with my children trying to explain why their grandparents act that way and say the horrible things that they heard. *"Why is grandpa so mean? Why does he want to kill himself? Why does he want to kill grandma?"*

As a teacher and my wife, having her medical practice here our name is extremely important to our professions and careers. Two students saw the four police cars at my house on Christmas Day and came to me at school to ask me *"if I was okay?"* His (our) name was in the Cranberry Eagle newspaper "Police Blotter", which I had to hide from my wife and children but people in my workplace saw it, which is extremely embarrassing. Our neighbors are very concerned for us (and themselves) after witnessing his actions on Christmas Day.

We have all addressed this issue in professional therapy including my sister who resides in Colorado. I had to reveal this situation to my employer since I filed a P.F.A. in case of him appearing at my school.

Upon advice of law enforcement, I have purchased a firearm and have attended multiple safety courses and instructions. I have a concealed weapon permit and a Utah license as well. I have attained these things only because of his threats and actions. I do not wish to carry a firearm, nor have I owned one previously.

At the initial hearing with the magistrate, ***** brought two unknown men with him to the court who stared at me throughout the proceedings and upon my departure, which I assume was to intimidate me. The actions, threats and assault on my home by *****. have greatly affected our lives and continues to disrupt my home and lifestyle. My wife and I are very concerned about how we are going to handle next year's Christmas planning and we both agree we do not want to be in our home. We will probably travel so we will not have to be in our home.

2. I received lacerations on my elbow and shoulder from his finger nails which were witnessed and documented by the Cranberry

Township Police and my physician. The emotional damage to my children, wife and myself is immeasurable.

3. The actions of ***** have made my workplace stressful and uncomfortable since his crime was observed by two of my students and that it was reported in the newspaper. I have no idea how many other students, parents and co-workers saw it. I was advised to replace a door with a steel security door and lock which I did not plan on doing. I feel like our home is on "lockdown" which continues to the current day. I will not leave my wife and daughter home alone. I no longer allow my mother at my home as a safety measure since she seems to be the source of his rage and anger.

4. I regularly visit and maintain my Grandmother's grave and have done so for over twenty years. ***** threatened me to *"never to go there again"*.

He has been physically violent and abusive with me throughout my childhood and threatened me with physical violence on Christmas Day. He has been physically violent and abusive to my mother in front of me on multiple occasions throughout my childhood. He has several friends who are violent, convicted felons and he readily has access to firearms. I have seen firearms in his home. So, yes, I am very affected by his statements and crimes.

Thank you for this opportunity and for everything that has been provided to me by the court and legal system of Cranberry Township and Butler County. I am very pleased and satisfied with the support and professionalism of everyone who has been involved throughout this process.

Thank you very much for your time and assistance,

Most Sincerely,

James Dennis Lucot JR.

When I discovered this list, I realized there was a name for this:

"12 Life-Impacting Symptoms Complex PTSD Survivors Endure"

By Lily Hope Lucario

1. Deep fear of Trust.
2. Terminal Aloneness
3. Emotional Regulation
4. Emotional Flashbacks
5. Hypervigilance About People
6. Loss of Faith
7. Profoundly Hurt Inner Child
8. Helplessness and Toxic Shame
9. Repeated Search for a Rescuer
10. Dissociation
11. Persistent Sadness and Being Suicidal
12. Muscle Armoring

The "Christmas Letter" (2017):

My father mailed this to me violating the P.F.A. resulting in an additional sentence of six-months' probation added to the previous sentence.

(Note: Six of the seven of my relatives on this list were deceased.)

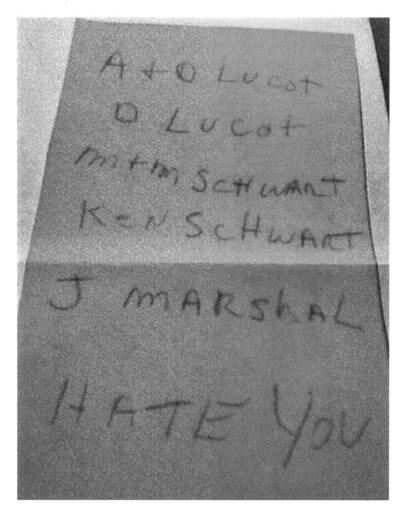

The Pitch, Hit and Run plaque:

(This had nothing to do with baseball and everything about trying to believe in myself.)

The Chain Link (2016):

I took six links of chain and cut a section out to symbolize that I am breaking the abusive history of my past for my wife and children. I made six of them for my family, my sister and two friends that helped and supported me. When I was visiting my son in college I saw the one I gave to him. He hung it on his bulletin board in his freshman dorm room.

The Steel Reinforced Door and Deadbolt Lock (2017)

This is the door I installed after my daughter told me that she had nightmares that my father might come back to our home. The previous door was mostly glass windows.

Resources:

National Suicide Prevention Lifeline 1-800-273-8255

www.healingfromcomplextraumaandptsd.com

http://stigmafighters.com/lilly-hope-lucario/

https://themighty.com/u/lilly-lucario/

isurvive.org

CPTSD Suffers and Support Group – Facebook

National Association of Adult Survivors of Child Abuse
http://www.naasca.org/

https://psychiatry.pitt.edu/research/participate-research

https://www.nami.org/Learn-More/Mental-Health-Conditions/Posttraumatic-Stress-Disorder/Support

https://www.childhelp.org/child-abuse/

https://www.childwelfare.gov/pubs/factsheets/whatiscan/

https://www.helpguide.org/articles/abuse/child-abuse-and-neglect.htm

https://www.healthychildren.org/English/safety-prevention/at-home/Pages/What-to-Know-about-Child-Abuse.aspx

https://www.doyouyoga.com/

how-to-combat-ptsd-with-yoga-91123/

Me at 2 and me at 15 years old:

I wish the smiles could have continued...

ABOUT THE AUTHOR

JAMES LUCOT JR. TEACHES HIGH SCHOOL A.P. U.S. GOVERNMENT and U.S. History. He also created a Holocaust Studies course that he teaches at a community college in the Pittsburgh area. He began he professional career as a registered nurse but made the career change to pursue his lifelong passion of history. When school is not in session he volunteers at his children's school and multiple veteran's programs including Honor Flight Pittsburgh. He has coordinated a History Roundtable for 20 years bringing history makers, veterans and Holocaust survivors to his community. He enjoys woodworking, photography and reading. His personal academic research is the Holocaust which have taken him to Poland and Israel on educational studies. He received a B.S.N. from Duquesne University, an M.S.A. from the University of Notre Dame and Pennsylvania State Education Certificate from Robert Morris University. He currently is working on a Master's in Holocaust and Genocidal Studies at Gratz College.

CPSIA information can be obtained
at www.ICGtesting.com
Printed in the USA
BVHW080254111218
535235BV00014B/456/P